Chess for Kids

How to Play and Win

Richard James

A HOW TO BOOK

ROBINSON

ROBINSON

First published in Great Britain in 2010 by Right Way
an imprint of Constable & Robinson Ltd

Reprinted in 2015 by Robinson

A CIP catalogue record for this book
is available from the British Library.

ISBN: 978-0-7160-2254-1

Printed and bound in China by C&C Offset Printing Co. Ltd.

Robinson
An imprint of
Little, Brown Book Group
Carmelite House
50 Victoria Embankment
London EC4Y 0DZ

An Hachette UK Company
www.hachette.co.uk

www.littlebrown.co.uk

How To Books are published by Robinson, an imprint of Little, Brown Book
Group. We welcome proposals from authors who have first-hand experience
of their subjects. Please set out the aims of your book, its target market and its
suggested contents in an email to Nikki.Read@howtobooks.co.uk

Chess
for Kids

About the Author

Richard James has been teaching chess to children since the 1970s and has worked with many future Grandmasters and International Masters. Richard is the webmaster of chessKIDS academy, a website pioneering online interactive chess instruction for young children: www.chesskids.com

Acknowledgements

Thanks to ChessBase (www.chessbase.com) for providing the chess fonts used in the diagrams, and to David Mostyn for his cartoons.

Contents

FOREWORD FOR PARENTS AND TEACHERS

This book is part of a multi-media project teaching chess to young children. On the chessKIDS website (www.chesskids.com) you will find a wide range of resources in the form of interactive lessons, video lessons, quizzes, worksheets and chess computers which will play various mini-games at different levels as well as complete chess games. You will also find more detailed advice for both parents and teachers on how to make the most of this book.

Chess is essentially an adult game, not a children's game: a game which can only be mastered with a seriousness of approach allied to an intense focus. Having said that, it is also a game which many children enjoy playing, at which some children can excel, and which, if it is taught correctly, can lead to a wide range of educational and social benefits. But just spending half an hour or an hour a week at a school chess club will lead to very little benefit and only a short-term interest in the game.

The Swiss psychologist Jean Piaget described four stages in the child's cognitive development. The sensorimotor stage (up to age 2) need not concern us here. In the pre-operational stage (ages 2 to 7), according to Piaget, children cannot use logical thinking. Children in this stage of development can learn how to set up the board, and the names and moves of the pieces, but would find understanding logical concepts such as checkmate and doing anything very much more than playing random moves difficult. Piaget's theories have been modified a lot over the years and we now know that some children can, given the talent and the right circumstances, play chess to a very high standard at the age of 7.

In the concrete operational stage (ages 7 to 12) children can think logically, but only in concrete rather than abstract terms. In this stage children will have no problem understanding the rules of chess but, typically, will find it hard to consider more than one aspect of the position at the same time, will be unaware of the positions of all the pieces on the board, and will struggle to find logical reasons for choosing between alternative moves. On the other hand, a few children at the higher end of the age range approach master standard.

In the formal operational stage (age 12 upwards) children are able to think logically and use abstract thought processes. Beginners in this age group can usually pick up the game quickly and start playing a full game. But children in the concrete operational stage need to learn slowly, in a step by step fashion. It is for children at or approaching this stage of development that this book is written.

That, then, is the pedagogical theory behind the book and the chessKIDS website. Children of this age (about 6 to 8) need short sharp lessons focusing on one big idea. Tell them, show them, let them do it themselves, repeat, reinforce, repeat again, reinforce again, then test that they have understood the lesson. Only then do you move onto the next lesson. As far as chess goes, the skills are not only those directly to do with chess, but skills involving thinking in different ways, observation and visualization.

Here in the UK, what happens all too often (and I spent years doing it myself) is that we show them the moves one week and expect them to play in a tournament the following week. To me, this is very much like teaching children addition, subtraction, multiplication and division all in one go and then expecting them to do advanced calculus.

There's no need to hurry. Your children have another 80 years or so to play chess. If you leave something a bit too late they can easily catch up, but if you try to do something too soon and they find it too hard, back off and wait a few months. Showing your frustration will not help. At the time of writing, the Norwegian Magnus Carlsen (born 30 November 1990) is the world's highest rated player. Magnus, who comes from a chess playing family, learnt the moves at about 5½ or 6, but found the game too hard at first, only returning to the board when he was 8.

You can approach the game at many levels. Perhaps you're reading this book because Uncle Fred likes a game when he comes round at Christmas and it would be nice if young Johnny or Jenny could play him. That's absolutely fine. You'll find all you need in these pages – and you may well also find that Uncle Fred doesn't know all the rules himself. Try him on the en passant rule and see what happens!

Maybe Johnny and Jenny's school has a chess club. You've read somewhere that Chess Is Good For You and would like them to join. Fine, but they are likely to forget or misunderstand anything they're taught there unless it is reinforced at home, which is where you come in. If you really want them to benefit from chess you'll need to work with them at home as well, and our multi-media chess resources will make that fun for them.

You might be more ambitious and would like to give Johnny and Jenny the chance to play at a higher level, maybe even to play internationally and, if they're good enough, become International Masters or Grandmasters. This book will only start them on that road, but it will ensure they make a good start. It's said that it takes 10,000 hours of serious practice to excel at an activity such as chess, and, up to a point, the sooner you start the better. So we're talking about several hours a week, maybe even 10–20 hours a week if you want them to reach the very top. But the problem is that at this age it's your decision, not theirs, and, if they want their life to take a different route they might not thank you for it later. And, while they may have the chess playing skills to compete at a high level, they will not necessarily have the emotional skills to go with them.

In this book you will find the rules of chess, or at least all the rules you need to know to play casually (serious tournament competitors will need a bit more) along with some very basic advice on tactics and strategy. Particular attention is given to the specific cognitive skills you need for chess, including the three questions you need to ask yourself every move: what good moves can I play, what good moves can my opponent play, and is the move I want to play safe? Without these you are not really a chess player, but young children find them very hard to master. The first part of the course involves playing mini-games with a few pieces on each side. The basic skills are best developed in such games rather than in complex positions from "big chess" with a lot of pieces on the board and many possibilities for both sides.

You will also find advice on developing memory and focus, decision making, following a plan and much else. Beyond that, the story line, Socratic teaching method and subversive humour give children the chance to discuss a wide range of topics with their parents and teachers: differences between boys and girls, attitudes towards competition and aggression, winning and losing, success and failure, relationships between adults and children. On the website there is also information about how the material can link up to subjects on the school curriculum.

You may ask why war is used as a metaphor for chess. The original form of the game was developed in India in about AD 600 as a representation of the type of army in use there at that time, so chess really is a war game, not just an abstract strategy game. Understanding this can be helpful in understanding what's happening on the board. A search for quotes by leading players and a glance at titles of chess books will reveal that its most successful practitioners see the game very much in terms of aggression, violence and killing, albeit in a very quiet environment with a strict code of etiquette. "Chess is a sport – a violent sport" claimed Marcel Duchamp, who was an international chess player as well as one of the most influential artists of the twentieth century. The American (ex-USSR) Grandmaster Boris Gulko tells his pupils that chess is a game for hooligans.

The start of the concrete operational stage of development is also the age at which boys and girls tend to develop separate personalities, and many boys (and some girls) develop an interest in fighting, weapons, wars and soldiers. This is a normal and healthy phase of child development and, as long as it is talked about, and channelled purposefully and constructively through both physical and mental activities, will have no long-term ill effects. As Konrad Lorenz pointed out, aggression is a completely natural instinct, and, of itself, neither bad nor good. The course outlined in this book and on the chessKIDS website is designed to use this in two ways: by employing fantasy violence to grab children's interest and make them laugh, and to provide a starting point for discussions with parents and teachers about violence and killing.

Finally, although school chess clubs are often loud and chaotic, the world of "real" competitive chess is quiet and organized. For those children on the autistic spectrum who perhaps excel in subjects such as maths or computing, who can focus intently on their special interests, and who require a low stimulation environment, chess can be an ideal, and sometimes life-changing hobby, a world in which they can meet and make friends with like-minded people, and can be valued purely by the moves they make on the chessboard. Those are the children with whom I feel the most affinity, and they are the reason I do what I do.

If you have any questions on anything in this book I can be contacted by email via www.chesskids.com or www.richardjames.org.uk.

INTRODUCTION

"Sam and Alice, you're always fighting. Go home before you get into any more trouble. If I see you fighting again you'll be in detention every afternoon this week."

On the way home they passed a door with a sign outside.

JOIN THE ARMY
APPLY WITHIN

"Should we go in, Alice?" asked Sam.

"I'm not so sure," his twin sister replied. "Do you think Mum and Dad would like it?"

"Who cares about them? If we join the army we'll be allowed to fight, won't we?"

"I suppose so. If you really want to, I'll come with you."

*   *   *   *   *

"Hello. We'd like to join the army."

"We're looking for the smartest and bravest kids on the planet. Are you smart and brave?"

"I'm the bravest kid on the planet," said Sam.

"And I'm the smartest," added Alice. "But why do you want kids to join the army?"

"We've picked up a message from outer space. Evil aliens from the planet Caïssa are planning to invade Earth. We need to find the smartest and bravest kids on the planet to fight them."

"Why kids? Why not grownups?" asked Alice.

"Kids are much smarter than grownups, and much braver as well. Grownups are scared of aliens, you know."

"What do you think, Sam? Should we join?"

"Sounds like a lot more fun than school."

"If you want to join the army you must come here every week after school. But, whatever you do, don't tell any grownups about the aliens."

"We'll see you next week, then," said Sam.

*   *   *   *   *

"I've just thought of something, Alice. We need an excuse for why we're late home from school."

"I know, Sam. Tell Mum we've joined the chess club. Chess is a nice quiet game. Grownups like that."

CHAPTER 1
THE INFANTRY

"WE'VE COME for our first lesson. When can we start fighting?" asked Sam.

"Be patient, Sam. There are some things you need to know first.

"The battle with the Caïssans will be fought under the rules of Intergalactic Warfare. In Intergalactic Warfare there are two armies, White and Black. White starts the battle and then the two armies take it in turns to move. That means that you have time to think about what you're going to do next. So you have to be very smart as well as very brave to win a battle. The Caïssans call it CHESS, so that's what we'll call it as well."

"Is that the battlefield over there? Why is half of it red?"

"It's stained with the blood of fallen warriors, Sam. One day it will be stained with your blood as well."

"It'll serve you right for being so mean to me," said Alice.

"Cool," said Sam. "I'm not scared."

"That's enough. Any more from you and I'll knock your heads together. This isn't school, you know. I'm not going to be nice to you like your teachers.

"Stop arguing for a minute and look at the battlefield. There are 8 rows and 8 columns, each with 8 squares. That makes 64 squares in total. If you're good at maths you'll know that 8 x 8 = 64.

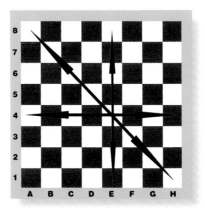

"The squares are light and dark: we also call the light squares the WHITE SQUARES and the dark squares the BLACK SQUARES. Even if they're red.

"One very important thing to remember is that the corner square nearest your RIGHT HAND must always be WHITE. WHITE ON THE RIGHT – remember!

"The 8 rows of squares on the battlefield are called RANKS and the 8 columns of squares are called FILES. You can also make diagonal lines containing squares of the same colour. These, amazingly enough, are called DIAGONALS.

"If you look closely you'll see some letters and numbers round the outside of the battlefield. The letters go from a to h and the numbers from 1 to 8. Each square has a name made up of the letter of its FILE followed by the number of its RANK. Like a1, e4 or h8."

One very important thing to remember is that the corner square nearest your RIGHT HAND must always be WHITE.

"Now you know all about the battlefield it's time for your first battle."

"Sounds good," said Sam. "Do I get to kill any aliens?"

"Come out to the battlefield and I'll show you what you have to do. In this battle you're going to join the INFANTRY. In chess the INFANTRY are called PAWNS."

"Prawns?" asked Sam.

"Not prawns, PAWNS," corrected Alice.

"Each army starts with EIGHT PAWNS. The WHITE PAWNS start from a2 to h2 and the BLACK PAWNS start from a7 to h7.

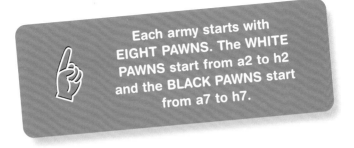

Each army starts with EIGHT PAWNS. The WHITE PAWNS start from a2 to h2 and the BLACK PAWNS start from a7 to h7.

"Pretend you're a white pawn, Sam. Stand there on the e2 square. And Alice, you'll be a black pawn so go and stand on e7. Now Sam, as you are in charge of the white pieces,

you make the first move. And you have a choice. On your first move you can go forward either one or two squares. What do you want to do?"

"I'll go forward two squares. That puts me on e4, doesn't it?"

"Very good. Now, Alice, you have the same choice. One square or two?"

"I'll move forward one square. Now I'm on e6."

On its first move a pawn can go forward either one or two squares. After its first move it can only move one square forward.

"After your first move you can only move one square forward, so Sam now has to move to e5. And now there's nothing Alice can do."

"That doesn't seem very exciting," said Sam.

"Be patient, Sam. Now, Alice, suppose for a minute you're on d6, not e6. Now, in a game of chess, you could CAPTURE Sam."

"That's not fair," protested Sam.

"Wait a minute. If it was your move, Sam, you'd be able to CAPTURE Alice. Because pawns can CAPTURE by moving

ONE SQUARE DIAGONALLY FORWARDS. The enemy pawn is taken off the board and your pawn takes its place."

"Now how about taking part in a real battle? This is called CAPTURE THE FLAG. There's a flag at each end of the battlefield. The first army to get to the end CAPTURES THE FLAG and wins the game. You also win if you CAPTURE all the other side's army or if the other army has no moves.

Pawns can CAPTURE by moving ONE SQUARE DIAGONALLY FORWARDS.

"You're going to need guns for this. One for you, Alice, and one for you, Sam. If you capture your enemy you get to shoot them."

"Water guns! Great! This is going to be so much fun!" exclaimed Sam. "Who's going to start?"

"Ladies first!" said Alice. "I'll start. That means I'm the white army, doesn't it?"

"Well remembered! Alice, you start on e2 and, Sam, you go to c7. Now Alice, you can move forward either one or two squares."

"Two squares. It's nearer the end of the board," said Alice.

Sam moved two squares, to c5. Now they could only move one square forward each move. Alice moved to e5, Sam to c4, Alice to e6, Sam to c3, Alice to e7, Sam to c2 and Alice to e8.

"Loser!" shouted Alice, opening fire at Sam.

"Hey, that's not fair. I'm going first next time!" replied Sam.

"OK kids, this time Sam gets White. Sam, you start at e2 and Alice starts at e7."

"Cool! I'll move forward two squares, to e4," said Sam.

"And I'll move to e5," said Alice. "Now you can't move so I think I win. Enjoy the soaking!"

"I'll get you next time," said Sam. "Let's start again. I'll just move one square, to e3."

Alice stopped to think. If she moved two squares, to e5, Sam would win by moving to e4. So she moved to e6 instead. Sam had to move to e4, and Alice won by moving to e5.

"I think I get it now," said Alice. "I can always win if I copy your first move. If you move two squares I move two squares and if you move one square I move one square."

"It's my turn to get you," said Sam. "This time you go first."

"Very well, I'll start on e2 and you start on d7," said Alice. "I'm moving two squares, to e4."

"Hey, just a minute! If I copy your move this time you'll get me!" Sam thought for a bit. "So I'll move one square instead, to d6. Now you have to move to e5 and I get you. Yay! I win at last!" exclaimed Sam, opening fire.

"Let's start again," said Alice. "This time I'll move one square, to e3."

Sam thought again. Should he move to d6 or d5? Finally he made up his mind. "I'm moving to d5. Now you have to move to e4 and again I win. So in this game I can win if I do the opposite to you. If you move two squares I move one square, and if you move one square I move two squares."

"For your homework I want you to practise playing some more games like this. Try it out with two pawns against one, or two against two and see what happens. If you look on our website you'll find a lot more about how to play these games."

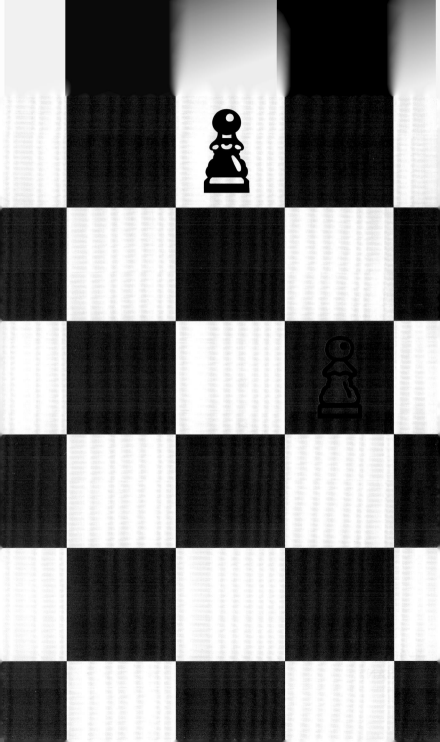

CHAPTER 2
EN PASSANT

"THERE'S ONE more rule you have to learn before you can take part in a real pawn battle. This is a VERY hard rule. Only the most intelligent kids in the world can understand it. Alice, you're a white pawn. I want you to stand over there on e5. Sam, you go and stand on d7. Note that you're on the NEXT FILE to Alice and that you haven't moved yet. Now tell me this, Sam. What would happen if you moved forward one square?"

"Alice would shoot me, wouldn't she?"

"Correct! Now you might want to move two squares to avoid getting shot. But there's a special rule called the EN PASSANT rule (it's French for IN PASSING) which says that, if she chooses, Alice can shoot Sam while he PASSES the d6 square. Try it out now. Sam, you try to move to d5, and, Alice, shoot Sam while he's PASSING the d6 square."

"That's so unfair," complained Sam. "Can I have a go next?"

"Very well, Sam. You go and stand on d4. Where does Alice need to stand so that you can shoot her next move?"

"Let's see. On e2, I think," said Sam. "Or c2," added Alice.

"Right, Alice, you go and stand on c2. Can you avoid being shot?"

"If I move to c3, Sam will shoot me. So I could move to c4 instead. But Sam can hit me while I'm PASSING c3, can't he?"

"Very good. I think you've got it. The rule is this. If you have a pawn on YOUR FIFTH RANK (if you're White that's RANK number 5, and if you're Black that's RANK number 4) and your opponent moves a pawn on the NEXT FILE TWO SQUARES then you can TAKE the enemy pawn just as you would if he moved one square, while he's PASSING the first square. But you can only do this on your next move. If you wait any longer it's too late."

> If you have a pawn on YOUR FIFTH RANK and your opponent moves a pawn on the NEXT FILE TWO SQUARES then you can TAKE the enemy pawn just as you would if he moved one square, while he's PASSING the first square.

"I don't think I can remember that," said Sam.

"If I write down the words I could remember it like lines in a play," said Alice.

"If you can't remember the words, Sam, try playing it out like a movie in your head. And remember getting soaked when Alice fired her gun at you."

"I'll try," said Sam, uncertainly.

"Now you know enough for your first real pawn battle. This is a game of CAPTURE THE FLAG with eight pawns on each side. Sam and Alice, you're both in the white army.

Sam, you start on e2 and, Alice, you start on c2. You won't need your water guns this time. Take these instead."

The battle started with Sam moving from e2 to e4 and the black pawn on d7 moving to d5.

"I can take him, can't I?" asked Sam. He opened fire and the enemy soldier fell to the ground. Sam took his place on d5.

The black pawn on h7 moved to h5, and Alice joined in, moving from c2 to c4. Next, the black pawn on g7 moved to g5 and Alice moved up to c5, alongside Sam. Now the black pawn on e7 moved forward one square, to e6.

Sam saw that he was in danger and rushed forward to d6, but it was too late. The soldier on c7 took aim and Sam fell to the ground.

"What's happened?" screamed Alice. "Sam's been shot. Is he dead?"

"No time to think about that. You can get your revenge."

"I can't do it. He might get hurt."

"This is war, Alice. That's what happens in war."

Reluctantly, Alice shot the enemy soldier and took his place on d6. Then she looked ahead and saw that the path was clear. In two moves she'd be able to CAPTURE THE FLAG and win the battle for the white army.

*   *   *   *   *

"I didn't see him," said Sam. "We lost, didn't we? And it was all my fault."

"Actually, we won," said Alice. "We won because you were a hero. You gave up your life so that your army could win the battle. And we were only using stun guns, so there was no harm done."

"Hey, why don't we play this game with Dad when we get home?" asked Sam.

"Good idea, kids, but remember you should always let grownups win. Grownups sometimes cry when they lose, you know. And if they don't cry, they get angry."

"Dad's too easy," said Alice. "Isn't there anyone better we could play?"

"Well, Alice. If you go onto our website you can take on the great American general, FISHY BOBBER. FISHY will even give you a start if you want, but of course you still have to let him win.

"And go through our online lesson on the EN PASSANT capture EVERY DAY until you remember it. FISHY will use it against you, so you have to make sure you know it really well."

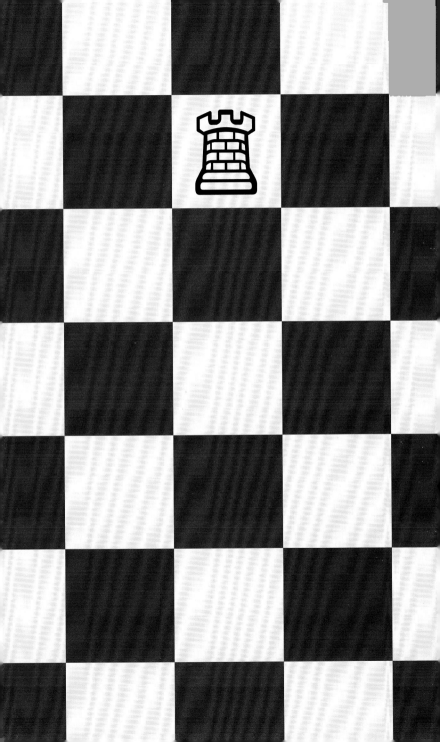

CHAPTER 3

THE CHARIOT

"THAT SKATEBOARD over there looks really good," said Sam. "When can I have a go?"

"Not for a long time yet, Sam. It's much too dangerous. But I can show you how it works if you like.

"In battle they're CHARIOTS but in chess, remember, they're called ROOKS. Don't call them CASTLES whatever you do! Each player has TWO ROOKS. They start in the corners: the WHITE ROOKS on a1 and h1 and the BLACK ROOKS on a8 and h8. ROOKS move FORWARDS, BACKWARDS and SIDEWAYS as far as they want as long as there's nothing in their way. You know that PAWNS MOVE and CAPTURE in different ways, but ROOKS, like all the other pieces in your army, MOVE and CAPTURE the

same way. If there's an enemy piece in the ROOK'S path your ROOK can CAPTURE it by moving to its square and taking it off the board.

"On an empty chessboard a ROOK can move to 14 squares so it's much more powerful than a PAWN."

"That's easy," said Sam. "I don't see why I couldn't ride one."

"They're very hard to control, Sam. You can watch a ROOK battle instead, though. This is a game of CAPTURE THE FLAG in which one ROOK battles against five PAWNS.

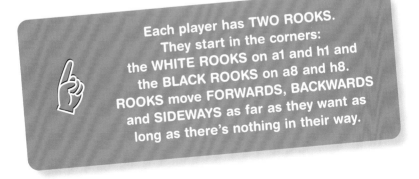

Each player has TWO ROOKS.
They start in the corners:
the WHITE ROOKS on a1 and h1 and
the BLACK ROOKS on a8 and h8.
ROOKS move FORWARDS, BACKWARDS
and SIDEWAYS as far as they want as
long as there's nothing in their way.

There's one more rule you need to know. If a PAWN reaches the end, the enemy ROOK has one move to take him before he CAPTURES THE FLAG."

There were five black footsoldiers in place and a white chariot on h1 awaiting its rider. Without thinking, Sam rushed up to the chariot, jumped onboard and started moving forwards.

"Come back," shouted Alice. "It's too dangerous." But it was too late.

It seemed like a good idea for Sam to ride the chariot to h7 where he'd be attacking all the enemy soldiers. The black soldier on b7 advanced two squares, to b5. Sam turned right, knocking down the soldier on f7. As the black soldier continued his advance down the b-file Sam knocked down the other soldiers like a row of skittles. The black soldier moved to b4 and Sam knocked down the man on e7. The black soldier moved to b3 and Sam knocked down the man on d7. Now Sam had lost control. The black soldier moved to b2 and Sam knocked down the man on c7. The black soldier reached the end of the battlefield on b1, CAPTURING THE FLAG as Sam crashed into the safety barrier.

Sam knocked down the other soldiers
like a row of skittles.

"That was exciting," said Sam. "I knocked down four men. Does that mean I won?"

"No, Sam. I'm afraid you lost. The man you didn't knock down CAPTURED THE FLAG."

"I couldn't help it."

"I think you could help it," said Alice. "You know your problem. You never stop and think before you do anything. Look here. This was when you knocked down the guy on c7. You have to knock down the b2 guy before he CAPTURES THE FLAG."

"Stop and think this time, Sam. What should you have done here?"

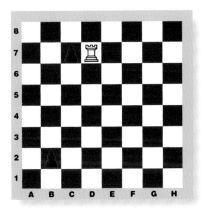

"I could move to d2 and take the b2 guy next move, couldn't I?"

"No, Sam. That's not going to work. After you've moved to d2 it's the black army's move. The soldier on b2 can still move to b1 and CAPTURE THE FLAG safely. Think again."

"I get it now. If I move to d1 instead, then I can knock him down when he gets to b1 but before he CAPTURES THE FLAG."

"You got there at last. Well done! So tell me kids, what did you learn from that?"

"You have to stop and think before you make a move," said Sam.

"Good. What do you have to think about?"

"You have to think about what the other guy's going to do next," said Alice.

"Absolutely right. And now it's time for you to think about going home before you have any more accidents. Practise this game again during the week. You can also play some CAPTURE THE FLAG games at home, or on your computer against FISHY. Here are two more games you can play, using all the pawns. Try these out as well. You'll find advice on how to play these games well on our website."

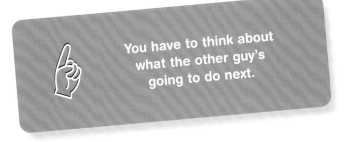

CHAPTER 4
THE ELEPHANT

"**I** DON'T LIKE the idea of riding one of those elephants," said Alice. "There's a long way to go if you fall off."

"You're just scared, Alice," said Sam. "They won't go very fast anyway. Here, I'll show you."

"No way, Sam. Not after what happened last time. You have to go back to being a pawn until you learn to do as you're told. And you're wrong, as well. These elephants are specially bred for intergalactic warfare. They go just as fast as chariots, but in a different way.

"In chess they're called BISHOPS. Each player starts with TWO BISHOPS. The WHITE BISHOPS start on c1 and f1, and the BLACK BISHOPS start on c8 and f8. On the

chessboard they move DIAGONALLY as far as they can go. Just like ROOKS they get blocked by friendly pieces and can CAPTURE enemy pieces by landing on their square and taking them off the board.

"A BISHOP in the middle of an empty board can move to 13 squares, but a BISHOP in the corner can only move to 7 squares.

"What do you notice about all the squares a BISHOP can move to?"

"They're all the same colour," said Alice.

Each player starts with TWO BISHOPS. The WHITE BISHOPS start on c1 and f1, and the BLACK BISHOPS start on c8 and f8. On the chessboard they move DIAGONALLY as far as they can go.

"That's right. Each player starts with a BISHOP on a WHITE SQUARE and a BISHOP on a BLACK SQUARE. Those BISHOPS will stay on the same colour square all the way through the battle.

"How would you like to join in a battle between a white BISHOP and three black PAWNS? Sam, I'm afraid you have to be a PAWN. Alice, would you like to be the BISHOP, or a PAWN along with Sam?"

"I'm not ready to ride the elephant yet," said Alice. "I think I'll be a PAWN if you don't mind."

So the battle started. The white elephant was on f1. Alice started on a7 and Sam on b7, with Charlie, another trainee, on c7. The elephant moved one square along the diagonal, from f1 to g2.

Sam looked along the diagonal. "I'm in danger, aren't I? I'd better move to b6. If we all keep on black squares there's no way the elephant will be able to get us."

The elephant moved along the long diagonal from g2 to c6, right in front of Charlie.

"Charlie can't move," said Sam, "and if I move I'll get taken. Alice, you have to move."

"I don't want to move too far," thought Alice. "I'd better move one square, to a6."

The elephant moved to b7, putting Alice in danger.

"You've got to move again, Alice," shouted Sam. Alice again moved one square, from a6 to a5. The elephant returned to the c6 square.

"I'm not moving," said Sam. "He'll get me if I move to b5."

"I'm not moving either," said Alice. "He'll get me if I move to a4. Anyway I moved last so it's your turn now."

"No way," said Sam. "Ladies first, remember."

A fight broke out and, using his greater strength, Sam pushed Alice forward to a4. The elephant advanced, trampling Alice into the ground.

Using his greater strength,
Sam pushed Alice forward to a4.

"Sorry, Alice," said Sam, "but I had no choice. Now, Charlie, you must move to c5. We'll still be safe if we stay on black squares." Charlie moved to c5 and the elephant moved to b5. (See next page.) Now Charlie had to move to c4 where he was trampled by the elephant. Finally, Sam saw what was

happening but it was much too late. He had to move to b5 where he too was trampled. The elephant had won the battle.

"You set us up, didn't you?" complained Sam. "You set it up so that we'd lose."

"Not true. I set it up so that you could win. But there was an error in your thinking. You thought you'd be safe from the elephant by keeping on black squares. The problem with that is that one of you had to move onto an unsafe white square. Your mistake was your first move. If Charlie had moved one square on the first move instead of you, you'd have won the battle with best play. It's a hard one, I know, but try it out again when you get home and see for yourselves. You can also try out some CAPTURE THE FLAG games with all the pawns to give you lots of practice with using the bishop."

CHAPTER 5

THE QUEEN

"I'VE BEEN thinking," said Sam.

"You've been thinking, have you? That makes a change."

"That's exactly what I mean. You're horrid to me all the time. I got shot. Then I crashed a chariot. Then I was trampled by an elephant. And every time you tell me it's all my fault. I've had enough. I'm quitting."

"Listen to me, Sam. Of course I'm mean to you. This is the army, not school. And the Caïssans are going to be a lot meaner to you than I am. I really don't want you to quit. You're one of the bravest kids I've ever seen, and you're pretty smart as well. The only problem I have with you is that you always do things without thinking first. Once you've worked round that you'll do really well. Tell you what, just watch Alice today. She's going to learn all about the QUEEN."

"Fine," said Sam. "Queens are for girls. I don't want to be a queen anyway. I expect they're really weak and stupid as well."

"Actually, Sam. You couldn't be more wrong. The QUEEN is the most powerful soldier in the army. Each army starts with just ONE QUEEN. The WHITE QUEEN starts on d1 and the BLACK QUEEN starts on d8, each on their own colour. You see that go-kart over there?"

"Great," exclaimed Sam, suddenly feeling happier. "I love go-karts. Can I have a go?"

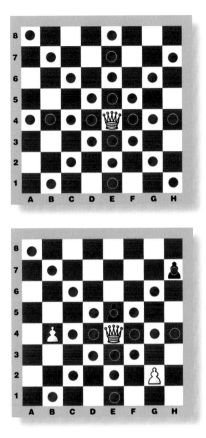

"Don't interrupt me, Sam. And, no, you can't have a go. You told me you were quitting. That go-kart can move in EIGHT directions. It can move forwards, backwards and sideways like the CHARIOT (the ROOK in chess) and diagonally like the ELEPHANT (the BISHOP in chess). So, in the centre of the board it can move to 27 squares – 14 like a ROOK and 13 like a BISHOP, and, in the corner, 21 squares – 14 like a ROOK and 7 like a BISHOP. And the GO-KART is what the QUEEN uses to travel across the battlefield."

Each army starts with just ONE QUEEN. The WHITE QUEEN starts on d1 and the BLACK QUEEN starts on d8.

"Now, Alice, in this CAPTURE THE FLAG battle you are the QUEEN in your GO-KART and you are battling against EIGHT PAWNS. Do you think you can win? You're White so you start."

"I'm not sure that I want to do this," said Alice. "They might get hurt if I knock them down."

"Don't worry about that, Alice. They're really brave so they won't cry too much. People get hurt in wars. You have to get used to it."

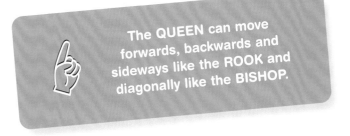

The QUEEN can move forwards, backwards and sideways like the ROOK and diagonally like the BISHOP.

Time stood still while Alice considered her first move. "Hurry up, Alice," shouted Sam. "We haven't got all day, you know. Why don't you hit the guy on d7?"

"There's no hurry, Sam. Don't forget that you take it in turns. It's sometimes a good idea to think carefully before making a move."

Alice moved forward and knocked down the soldier on d7. The enemy soldier on h7 moved to h5. Alice stopped to think again.

Alice moved forward and knocked down
the soldier on d7.

It's sometimes a good idea to think carefully before making a move and make sure it's safe.

"I could hit the soldier on c7 or the soldier on e7. I really can't make up my mind. This is so hard." Eventually she decided to turn right, hitting the enemy on e7. The soldier on h5 moved again, to h4.

"Now I have a choice again," thought Alice. "c7 or f7? Just a minute. If I move diagonally backwards I can hit the guy on h4. Perhaps I'd better do that before he gets to the end of the board."

Alice knocked down the soldier on h4 and now the soldier on g7 moved to g5.

"I'm under attack," said Alice to herself. "But I could take him. I've really got to think very carefully and make sure it's safe. Yes, I think it is safe so here goes."

A fourth black soldier fell to the ground and this time the soldier on c7 moved to c5.

Alice looked carefully at the battlefield and noticed that it was safe to hit the c5 guy. The soldier on f7 moved to f5.

Alice now worked out how she could win the battle. First she knocked down the enemy on a7. The soldier on f5 moved forward again, to f4, and Alice hit the soldier on b7. There was now only one black soldier left so he had to move from f4 to f3. Alice looked down the long diagonal and saw that she could hit him as well. With all eight black soldiers knocked out, Alice had won the battle.

"Well done, Alice. We made it easy for you to give you some confidence. Try playing it out against Sam on your chess set at home, but next time start with a black pawn on d6 rather than d7 to make it harder."

"Well done?" said Sam. "You tell her well done for doing something easy. Why do you never say anything nice to me?"

"You quit, Sam. I don't say anything nice to cowards. Winners never quit, and quitters never win. And, Alice, when you're sure you can take all eight black pawns with your QUEEN, try a CAPTURE THE FLAG game with a QUEEN and eight PAWNS each."

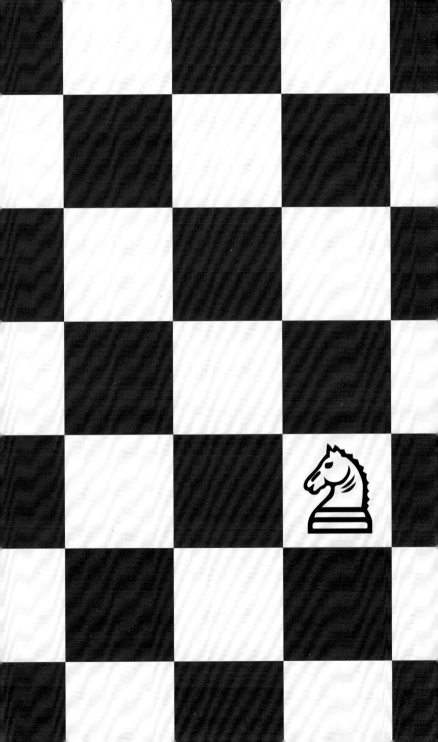

CHAPTER 6

THE CAVALRY

"I'VE ALWAYS wanted to learn to ride," said Alice. "Can I have a go at one of those horses?"

"You can, Alice, but you've got to be very careful. In a battle they're the cavalry: soldiers who ride horses into battle. In a game of chess they're called KNIGHTS. Each army has TWO KNIGHTS at the start of the battle. The WHITE KNIGHTS are stationed at b1 and g1, and the BLACK KNIGHTS are stationed at b8 and g8.

"They don't move in a straight line like the other pieces you've seen. The KNIGHT move is like a letter L. You go two squares forwards, backwards or sideways like a ROOK, and then, in the same movement, one square round the corner. Tell me, what do you notice about the squares the KNIGHT can move to?"

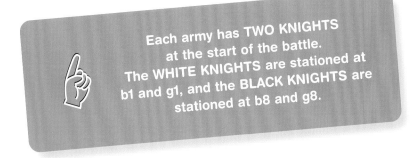

Each army has TWO KNIGHTS at the start of the battle. The WHITE KNIGHTS are stationed at b1 and g1, and the BLACK KNIGHTS are stationed at b8 and g8.

"They make a pattern which looks like a circle. Or a flower. Oh, and they're all the same colour."

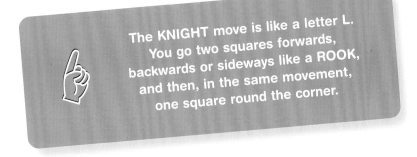

The KNIGHT move is like a letter L. You go two squares forwards, backwards or sideways like a ROOK, and then, in the same movement, one square round the corner.

"Very good, Alice. So a KNIGHT on a WHITE SQUARE always moves to a BLACK SQUARE and a KNIGHT on a BLACK SQUARE always moves to a WHITE SQUARE. And they capture the same way that they move, just like ROOKS, BISHOPS and QUEENS. A KNIGHT in the centre of the board can move to EIGHT squares, but a KNIGHT in the corner can only move to TWO squares.

"But there's another thing about KNIGHTS as well. Because they're horses they can JUMP. Unlike other pieces they can jump over anything in their way. So when you're riding a horse you have to be very careful that you don't fall off."

"That sounds really hard," said Alice. "I think I'm going to need a lot of practice."

"Good idea. What I want you to do is this. Get up on the horse on a1 and see how many moves it takes you to get to h8, the square in the opposite corner."

Because they're horses the KNIGHTS can JUMP. Unlike other pieces they can jump over anything in their way.

"Let's see now," thought Alice. "I can go forwards two squares and then one round the corner, that would take me to b3, wouldn't it?" So Alice moved to b3.

"That's fine. You had a choice between b3 and c2. Where are you going next?"

"I need to head for the far corner so perhaps I can move sideways two squares and then forward one. Then I'd be on d4."

"Keep going, Alice."

"I'll try going right two squares and up one again. That takes me to f5. Now I need to stop and think. I can nearly get to the corner by going up two and right one. That would take me to g7 but I think I might have a problem there. Perhaps I should go up two and left one, to e7."

"This looks fun," said Sam. "It's like a rodeo. When can I have a go?"

"You quit, didn't you, Sam?"

"I never said that. I've changed my mind anyway," Sam continued.

Meanwhile, Alice was working out the route to h8. "I can go right two squares, then back down one square, which will take me to g6. Yes, I think I can get to h8 from there." So Alice moved to g6, and then up two squares and right one square to h8. "How many moves was that?" she asked.

"You did it in six moves, Alice. Congratulations. Now, Sam, you said you wanted a go. Alice moved from a1 to h8 in six moves. It should be easy to do it in seven moves, shouldn't it?"

"Six moves is so easy even a girl can do it," laughed Sam. "So seven moves will be no problem at all."

"You want to bet on it, Sam? If you can't figure out how to do it you have to do a hundred press ups. Game on?"

"I can't lose this one," said Sam as he started off from a1.

Sam began by using the same route as Alice, from a1 to b3, d4 and f5. Now he went to g7, then to e8, then to f6. "That's six moves. Now all I have to do is move from f6 to h8."

"Sorry, Sam. You can't do it. You can reach g8 or h7 if you want, but not h8. Never mind, have another try."

Sam kept on trying for some time. He could get there in six moves or eight moves, but not seven moves.

Alice had been thinking. "I've worked out what's happening, Sam," she said. "Remember that a KNIGHT always moves from a WHITE SQUARE to a BLACK SQUARE and from a BLACK SQUARE to a WHITE SQUARE? You started on a BLACK SQUARE so on your first move you went to a WHITE SQUARE, then to a BLACK SQUARE. So you're always going to get to a WHITE SQUARE on your odd numbered moves and a BLACK SQUARE on your even numbered moves. So it's impossible to get from a1 to h8 in seven moves."

"You lost your bet, Sam. That's a hundred press ups."

"Hey! That's so unfair. You made me lose," protested Sam.

"No, Sam. You had a choice. You always have to make choices, both in chess and in life. You have to think first if you want to make the right choice."

"You must admit it's a good trick, Sam," said Alice. "We could try it on Dad when we get home."

"Yes," replied Sam. "I'd like to see him doing a hundred press ups."

"There are some more things I'd like you to do at home, kids. See how many pawns a KNIGHT can stop. What do you think? Two? Three? Four? Does it make any difference if the enemy pawns are on the next files to each other or on opposite sides of the board? When you've done that, try some CAPTURE THE FLAG games with KNIGHTS and PAWNS. Knights are tricky pieces so you'll need a lot of practice to get really good at using them."

CHAPTER 7
THE KING

"I CAN'T WAIT to find out what the KING does," said Sam. "I bet he's even better than the QUEEN."

"Well, each army starts with ONE KING. The WHITE KING starts on e1 and the BLACK KING on e8. The KING is the most important piece in the battle. But it's also the hardest piece to understand. You have to be really intelligent to understand what the KING does. And before you start you have to be really good at all the other pieces. You see, the KING is the general who commands his troops. He has to listen to all the other soldiers in his army and then decide on the best move."

"We're the most intelligent kids in the world," said Alice. "And we're really good at all the other pieces," added Sam.

"You will see that the KING moves just ONE square at a time in any direction."

The KING is the most important piece in the battle. He moves just ONE square at a time in any direction.

"That's not hard," interrupted Sam. "That's the easiest piece."

"But there's more to it than that. The KING CANNOT move to any square where he'd be taken by another piece. If you move any other piece to a square where it can be taken then your opponent can take it. But it's NOT POSSIBLE to move the KING to a square where he'd be taken. If you do so by mistake you have to go back and play another move instead. In this position the KING can't move to f3, f4 or f5 because of the rook, or to d4 or e5 because of the bishop."

"Cool. Can I have a go?" asked Sam.

"You can if you like but it's very dangerous. I think you'll probably need Alice to help you. To succeed in this task you have to cross a minefield. If you land on a square where an enemy soldier can take you, you'll be blown up. You start at e1 and you have to reach the far end of the minefield to survive.

"Before you start, Sam, what do you do before you cross the road?"

"Stop and look both ways," replied Sam.

"And what happens if you don't do that?"

"I get killed," replied Sam.

"Well, it's the same thing here. What you have to do is to look at every square you can move to and work out whether or not it's safe. Don't move until you're sure you've found a safe square. After all, we don't want you having your legs blown off, do we?"

"Right, I'll start off by moving to d2," said Sam.

"No," shouted Alice. "Look at the BISHOP on c1."

"Thanks, Alice. I'll try e2 instead."

"No: there's another BISHOP controlling e2. And there's a KNIGHT on c3 as well. I think f2's safe though."

"OK, I'll move to f2. And now along the diagonal to g3, I think."

"Don't forget that PAWNS take diagonally, Sam!"

"Oh yes, I forgot. I'll have to move to f3 instead. Now, is it safe to capture the PAWN on f4?"

"Just a minute Sam, I'll have a look. No, the BISHOP on c1 will get you. Try again."

"I think I can move to g4 safely. Yes, the PAWN on h3 is going the other way so he can't get me. Now where can I go from g4? Try moving forwards: f5? No – PAWN on e6: g5? Yes, that looks safe."

"Very good, Sam. You're getting the idea of it now. You've nearly reached the end of the board."

"Where can I go next? I'd like to go forward so I'll look at those moves first. Now, f6 isn't safe because of the KNIGHT on e8 or the PAWN on g7. What about g6? Yes, PAWNS can't take forwards so nothing can get me there. I've got to be really careful now, though. Again I'd like to move forwards. How about f7? I must stop and look at all the enemy pieces.

The PAWNS on e6 and g7 can't get me. The KNIGHT and the ROOK can't get me so it must be safe."

"You've just got to get to the eighth rank now, Sam. Whatever you do, be very careful."

"Right. I'll start by trying to move forwards. Can I take the KNIGHT on e8? No: the ROOK on h8 is stopping me. Come to think of it, he's also stopping me moving to f8 or g8. So I can't move forwards. I'll try moving sideways instead. Can I go to e7? The KNIGHT can't get me. The PAWN can't get me. Yes, e7 looks like it's safe. Can I move forwards from e7? I already know that e8 and f8 aren't safe so I must look at d8. I think it's safe. The BISHOP can't get me. The KNIGHT can't get me. The ROOK can't get me because the KNIGHT's in the way. Yes, I'm sure it's safe."

"Congratulations, Sam. You made it to the end of the battlefield without stepping on a mine."

"Phew!" exclaimed Sam. "For the first time I managed to do something right."

"Yes, although you needed some help from Alice at first. You know what? With a lot of practice you might just make a very good KING in the army."

"Can we play a proper battle yet?" asked Sam.

"Not quite yet. You still need to learn more about KINGS. But you could try some harder CAPTURE THE FLAG games to give you experience of using the different pieces together. Have a go at these."

CHAPTER 8
CHECK AND CHECKMATE

"Y OU' VE REALLY GOT to pay attention in this lesson, kids. This is the most important lesson you've had so far, and also the hardest lesson to understand.

"Now, Sam, you are the WHITE KING. I want you to stand there on e1. Alice, you're the BLACK QUEEN. Go and stand on c8. It's your move so I want you to move right down to c1. What do you see now?"

"I'm attacking Sam," said Alice.

"Correct. When you play a move that puts the enemy KING under ATTACK you should say 'CHECK' to warn your opponent. Sam, you are now IN CHECK. You remember from the last lesson that you are not allowed to move your KING to a square where he will be ATTACKED?"

"Yes," said Sam. "I remember. I had to avoid the mines."

"The next rule is that if the KING is IN CHECK, that is, it is ATTACKED by an enemy piece, you have to do something about it. The first thing you could do is MOVE to a safe square. How could you do that here, Sam?"

"Let me think. I can't move to d1 because Alice would be CHECKING me. I can't move to d2 either, can I? But I can move to e2 or f2 safely. And I can't move to f1."

"Very good, Sam. So here you can GET OUT OF CHECK by moving to either e2 or f2. The first way you can GET OUT OF CHECK is to MOVE YOUR KING TO A SAFE SQUARE.

"Now suppose I'm a WHITE ROOK on d5. This time you have another way to GET OUT OF CHECK. If you get me to move from d5 to d1 you will BLOCK THE CHECK. The second way you can GET OUT OF CHECK is to BLOCK

THE CHECK BY MOVING A PIECE BETWEEN THE CHECKING PIECE AND YOUR KING. You can only do this if you are IN CHECK from a QUEEN, a ROOK or a BISHOP.

"Next, I'll be a WHITE ROOK on c5. Now I can move to c1 and CAPTURE Alice – sorry, Alice. This is the third way you can GET OUT OF CHECK: CAPTURE THE PIECE THAT'S CHECKING YOU.

"Can KINGS make captures?" asked Sam.

"Yes, they CAPTURE the same way that they move. So if you're on e1 and Alice is on d1 then you can CAPTURE her just as long as you won't be IN CHECK on that square.

"So remember, if your KING is ATTACKED you are IN CHECK. If you are IN CHECK you must get out of CHECK at once. There are THREE WAYS of getting out of CHECK. MOVE to a safe square, BLOCK with another piece and CAPTURE the piece that's CHECKING you."

There are THREE WAYS of getting out of CHECK. MOVE to a safe square, BLOCK with another piece and CAPTURE the piece that's CHECKING you.

"What happens if you can't get out of CHECK?" asked Alice.

"Good question. Alice, you move back to c1. This time I'll be a BLACK ROOK on b2. Sam, Alice has just moved to c1. How are you going to get out of CHECK this time?"

"Do I get any other pieces in my army?" asked Sam.

"Not this time, I'm afraid, Sam. So, what are you going to do?"

"I still can't go to d1 or f1 because Alice will CAPTURE me. If I go to f2 or e2 you'll CAPTURE me. And if I go to d2 either of you will be able to CAPTURE me. I have no other men in my army, so I can't BLOCK the CHECK or CAPTURE Alice with another piece. But I have to move somewhere, don't I?"

"No, Sam. I'm afraid you can't move anywhere. As soon as Alice moves to c1 you're dead. If you reach a position where your KING is IN CHECK and you CANNOT GET OUT OF CHECK it's the end of the game. You've lost. Or, better, if you reach a position where the enemy KING is IN CHECK and he CANNOT GET OUT OF CHECK you've won. This is called CHECKMATE. You win the game by CHECKMATING the enemy king.

"So far you've been playing games of CAPTURE THE FLAG where you win by getting a pawn to the end of the battlefield safely. But REAL battles are very different. In a REAL game of chess you win by getting CHECKMATE: by CHECKING the enemy king in such a way that he CANNOT GET OUT OF CHECK.

"You can still go back and play CAPTURE THE FLAG games whenever you feel like it but you'll soon be ready to play a REAL game of chess."

If you reach a position where the enemy KING is IN CHECK and he CANNOT GET OUT OF CHECK you've won. This is called CHECKMATE. You win the game by CHECKMATING the enemy king.

"Can we play now?" asked Sam.

"First of all, you'll find some tests on the website to check that you understand all about CHECK and CHECKMATE."

"I hate tests," protested Sam. "They're boring."

"Only boring people get bored," replied Alice. "Interesting people can find a way to make anything interesting."

"The other thing you can do is switch on this computer."

"What does that do?" asked Sam.

"This button here is the hotline to Moscow where you can battle the famous Russian Grandmaster KASPY GARIKOV. This one takes you to New York where you can fight the famous American Grandmaster FISHY BOBBER: I think you've already met him. And, finally, the line to Holland where you can play the computer DEEP RED. They'll all play without some of their pieces to give you a start if you want. When you play them start at LEVEL 1, where you have your full army and they only have their king and pawns."

"What's a Grandmaster?" asked Alice.

"Grandmasters are the best players in the world, so be careful!"

"So are KASPY and FISHY the best players in the world?"

"Play them and find out for yourself. But remember one thing. They both get VERY angry when they lose, so you must always let them win!"

CHAPTER 9

STALEMATE AND OTHER DRAWS

"SAM, YOU'RE THE WHITE KING. Go and stand over there on a1, in the Naughty Corner!"

"What have I done wrong this time?" asked Sam. "Why am I always in trouble?"

"Just do as you're told, Sam, or you'll be in even more trouble. Alice, you're the black queen. I want you to go over to c2. Your move, Sam."

"I can't go to b1," said Sam. "I can't go to b2 either so I'll have to go to a2."

"Not so fast," said Alice. "I'll get you there as well."

"You've got a problem there, Sam, haven't you?"

"I can't move anywhere then," said Sam. "That means I lose, doesn't it?"

"No, Sam, you're not IN CHECK so you don't lose. When you were playing CAPTURE THE FLAG, if you couldn't move you lost, but in a real battle the rules are different."

"So I win then?" asked Sam.

"No! You don't lose, and you don't win either. The result is a DRAW. A position like this is called STALEMATE. IF YOU ARE NOT IN CHECK AT THE MOMENT AND YOU CANNOT MOVE YOUR KING OR ANY OTHER PIECE IT'S STALEMATE AND THE GAME ENDS AS A DRAW.

"Now suppose there's a white pawn over there on h4. Now it's NOT STALEMATE. You can't move but the pawn can move to h5. But if there's also a black king on h5 neither you nor your pawn can move so it's STALEMATE again."

"That sounds really complicated," said Sam. "I'm not sure I'll be able to remember it."

"You'll have to find a way, Sam, if you want to train to become a KING. If you can't remember the words, try to

IF YOU ARE NOT IN CHECK AT THE MOMENT AND YOU CANNOT MOVE YOUR KING OR ANY OTHER PIECE IT'S STALEMATE AND THE GAME ENDS AS A DRAW.

remember it as a picture instead. Imagine you're taking a photo of the position and then store it in your memory. Then set up some more STALEMATE positions and store those in your memory as well."

"I'll try," said Sam uncertainly.

"Here's another STALEMATE for you. Alice, you stay there on c2, and, Sam, I want you to go and stand on a3. At the moment the only square you can move to is b4. Now I'm the black king. If I stand on a square that stops you moving there – that CONTROLS b4 – then it's STALEMATE. I'll go

and stand on c4 and you'll see what I mean. It would still be STALEMATE if I was on c5, b5 or a5 instead. Take a picture of this position, Sam. Write the word STALEMATE on it and store it in your memory."

"Are there any other ways to DRAW a game of chess?" asked Alice.

"Yes, there are several other ways to DRAW a game. Suppose that all the other pieces get taken and each army ends up with just a KING left. There's no way a KING can CHECKMATE another KING. In fact a KING can't even CHECK another KING. If they were on the next square to each other they'd both be IN CHECK, which would be pretty silly. So, if that happens, you just stop play and call it a DRAW. The same thing happens if you end up with just KING AND BISHOP against KING or KING AND KNIGHT against KING, for instance. You can try it out for yourself if you like, but it's impossible to get CHECKMATE even if you try all day. So again you just call it a DRAW."

"What about KING and PAWN against KING?" asked Alice. "That must be a draw as well, because PAWNS are less powerful than KNIGHTS and BISHOPS."

"Actually that's not a DRAW, Alice, because there's something very special that a PAWN can do. You'll find that out in the next lesson."

"Is that all?" asked Sam. "Can we have a game now"?

"You're being impatient again, Sam. A real game of chess can last a long time so you wouldn't have time to finish. What would you do then?"

"Well, if the game was equal I suppose we could call it a draw," said Sam.

"Very good, Sam. Another way to DRAW a game of chess is just to agree a draw with your opponent because you think it's equal and neither of you has much chance to win."

"Are there any other ways to draw?" asked Alice.

"There are a couple of special rules, yes, but you don't need to know them unless you want to start playing in tournaments."

"Tournaments?" asked Sam. "What are they?"

"In chess tournaments there are dozens, sometimes hundreds, of kids just like you who all get to play chess together all day. The boys and girls who win the most games get prizes, maybe big trophies or sometimes even money! And everyone gets to make a lot of new friends who also enjoy playing chess."

"How cool is that!" exclaimed Sam. "We'd love to do that, wouldn't we, Alice?"

"Yes," agreed Alice. "That sounds really exciting. When will we be good enough to try?"

"Not for quite a long time yet. You still have a couple more rules to learn. And then you need to play a lot of games and solve a lot of puzzles."

"Should we play some games at home?" asked Alice.

"Yes. Play as many games as you can at home, and also play some more games against KASPY and FISHY where they only start with a few pieces.

"Here's some more advice for you. The best way to start your games is to move your e-pawn, the pawn in front of your king, two squares. By playing that move you open up

The best way to start your games is to move your e-pawn, the pawn in front of your king, two squares. By playing that move you open up lines for your queen and bishop to come out.

lines for your queen and bishop to come out. Try this. Play KASPY or FISHY when they only have their king and pawns. On your second move, bring your queen out along the diagonal to h5. Then use your queen to take as many enemy pawns as you can. Whatever you do, though, make sure you don't put your queen where she can get taken. Then you can bring your other pieces into play and try to get CHECKMATE. But don't forget to watch out for STALEMATE as well. If you don't CHECK your opponent, make sure he has a move to play next!"

CHAPTER 10

PAWN PROMOTION AND CASTLING

"**Y**OU SAID THERE WAS another special rule for pawns," said Alice. "Can you tell us about it?"

"Yes, thank you for reminding me, Alice. You remember that when you were playing CAPTURE THE FLAG you won the game by getting a pawn to the end safely. Well, in a real game of chess you win by getting CHECKMATE – but getting a pawn to the end safely will help you do this.

"When you get a PAWN to the end of the board you have to replace it with another piece of the same colour on the same square. You can choose a QUEEN, a ROOK, a BISHOP or a KNIGHT. Usually you'll choose a QUEEN because that's the most powerful piece. We call this PROMOTING A PAWN, or, if you choose a QUEEN, QUEENING A PAWN."

"It's just like *Alice Through the Looking Glass*, isn't it?" asked Alice. "And that's my name as well!"

"What happens if you've still got your queen?" asked Sam.

"Then you can get a second queen to go with it. If you get all eight pawns to the end you can get eight more queens to go with the one you started with. But two or three are usually enough to win easily. If you can't find another queen you can use an upside down rook instead."

"There are so many rules to remember," said Sam. "Have we learnt them all yet?"

"Very nearly, Sam. There's just one rule left to learn and it's a very important one especially for you. You know that if the KING gets CHECKMATED the enemy army wins the battle? And if you're the KING in the army fighting the Caïssans that means that YOU will be killed, the rest of the army will be put to death and the evil aliens will take over the planet.

"So there's a very special move which you can do once a game which will help make the KING safe. Here's how it works. Sam, you're the WHITE KING so go and stand on e1. Now I'm the WHITE ROOK on h1, and you will see that the

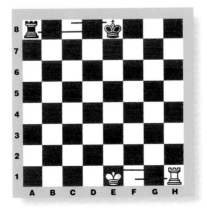

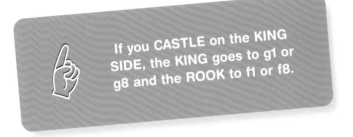

If you CASTLE on the KING SIDE, the KING goes to g1 or g8 and the ROOK to f1 or f8.

squares between us are empty. You move TWO squares towards me, leaving you on g1. IN THE SAME MOVE, I move one square past you to f1. This move is called CASTLING. So if you CASTLE on the KING SIDE, the KING goes to g1 or g8 and the ROOK to f1 or f8.

"You can do this on the other side as well. Go to e8, Sam, and this time I'll be a ROOK on a8. Again you move TWO SQUARES, this time to c8, and I again move one square past you, finishing on d8. So if you CASTLE on the QUEEN SIDE, the KING goes to c1 or c8 and the ROOK to d1 or d8.

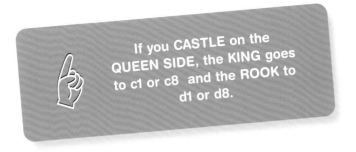

If you CASTLE on the QUEEN SIDE, the KING goes to c1 or c8 and the ROOK to d1 or d8.

"Do you understand so far?"

"I think so," said Sam, "but it seems a bit complicated."

"There's more, though. Go back to e1, Sam, and I'll go back to a1. Alice, you're the BLACK QUEEN. I want you to stand on e7. What do you notice, Sam?"

"I'm IN CHECK, aren't I?"

"That's right. And if you're IN CHECK you can't castle this move."

"Does it matter if you've been in check before?" asked Alice.

"No, as long as you got out of check another way rather than moving your king. You see, YOU CAN ONLY CASTLE IF YOUR KING AND ROOK HAVE NOT YET MOVED. And... YOU CANNOT CASTLE IF YOU ARE IN CHECK. OK?"

YOU CAN ONLY CASTLE IF YOUR KING AND ROOK HAVE NOT YET MOVED. And... YOU CANNOT CASTLE IF YOU ARE IN CHECK.

"I think so," said Sam and Alice together.

"Now, Alice, I want you to move from e7 to c7. Why can't you CASTLE here, Sam?"

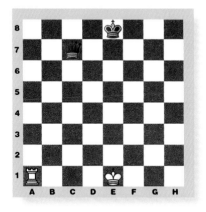

"If I move to c1 I'd be IN CHECK, wouldn't I?" replied Sam.

"Very good. So… YOU CANNOT CASTLE IF YOU WOULD END UP IN CHECK. Finally, Alice, move from c7 to d7, please.

YOU CANNOT CASTLE
IF YOU WOULD END UP
IN CHECK.

"It LOOKS like White can CASTLE here, but there's another rule. YOU CANNOT CASTLE IF YOUR KING WOULD CROSS A SQUARE WHICH IS ATTACKED BY AN ENEMY PIECE. And here, Sam, if you were to CASTLE you would have to pass the d1 square which Alice is attacking from d7. So in this position you CANNOT castle."

"Phew! Is that it?" asked Sam.

"Yes, you now know all the rules you need to play a complete game of chess. If you can show me you've remembered them all, that you understand CHECK, CHECKMATE and STALEMATE, CASTLING, PAWN PROMOTION and EN PASSANT you're ready to go!"

"EN PASSANT!" exclaimed Alice. "I'd nearly forgotten that one."

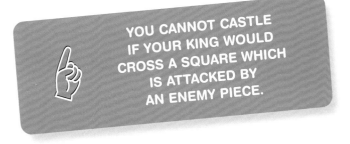

YOU CANNOT CASTLE
IF YOUR KING WOULD
CROSS A SQUARE WHICH
IS ATTACKED BY
AN ENEMY PIECE.

"When you play FISHY or KASPY, or when you play each other, try to CASTLE as quickly as you can. Move your e-pawn, then move your knight on g1 to f3 and move out your bishop on f1. Then you'll be ready to CASTLE on the KING SIDE."

"I'll try to remember that," said Sam. We could also try to PROMOTE some pawns as well, couldn't we?"

"Yes. That's also a good idea. If you have a QUEEN and a ROOK, or, even better, two QUEENS and the enemy KING is on the edge of the board you'll be able to get CHECKMATE easily. Put one of your pieces on the next line to the edge of the board to stop the KING escaping, then bring your other piece onto the same line as the KING.

"Look at the position below. You can start by moving your ROOK to a7. Black has to move his KING to d8 and next move you move your QUEEN to b8 which is CHECKMATE."

"Could we do it the other way round as well?" asked Alice.

"Good question. You're right: that's just as good. Move your QUEEN to b7 and then move your ROOK to a8. It's still CHECKMATE."

CHAPTER 11

THE VALUES OF THE PIECES

"ARE YOU GOOD AT MATHS, Sam?"

"Yes. I'm top of the class. Why?" replied Sam.

"In every battle there will be times when you have to decide which pieces to trade off. Maybe one or more of your guys might get killed in exchange for one or more guys from the other army. As the KING it's your job to decide when you should trade off pieces. To help you do this we give every piece a value. Which do you think is the weakest piece in your army?"

"The PAWN?" asked Sam. "It can only move one or two squares at a time."

"But when it gets to the end it can turn into a QUEEN. Then it becomes very strong," added Alice.

"You're both right. Most of the time the PAWNS are the weakest guys in your army. We say they are worth ONE POINT. Next up are the KNIGHT and the BISHOP. They're both worth THREE POINTS. Then comes the ROOK, which

1 point   5 points

3 points   9 points

3 points   the game

is worth FIVE POINTS. The most powerful piece in your army is the QUEEN, which is worth about NINE POINTS. Sometimes a bit more, but for the moment we'll call it nine."

"What about the KING?" asked Sam. "You've missed him out. I want to know how much I'm worth."

"You're priceless, Sam! There's no need to give KINGS a value because they never get captured. Remember that both KINGS stay on the board all the way through the game. In terms of fighting power the KING is worth about three points but for most of the battle he has to remain safe rather than join in the fighting in case he gets CHECKMATED.

"You have to know this as well, Alice, because as well as being the strongest fighter in the army you also have to advise the KING and help him make the decisions. In this position you are White. The white KNIGHT can CAPTURE the black ROOK but if he does so he'll be CAPTURED by the black KING. Do you think White should make the CAPTURE?"

"I don't think so," answered Alice. I don't want to lose my KNIGHT. They're the only pieces that can jump."

"Alice, suppose I had five chocolates and you had three chocolates. Would you like to do a swap?"

"Yes, of course. I love chocolates," replied Alice.

"And suppose I had £5,000 and you had £3,000. Would you like to do a swap then?"

"Of course I would," replied Alice.

"Well, it's the same thing. ROOKS are better than KNIGHTS, even though they can't jump. That's why they are worth FIVE POINTS and KNIGHTS are only worth THREE POINTS. You won't understand why yet, but the most important thing to think about is making sure that your army is bigger and stronger than the other guy's army. In a battle between two good players, even an advantage of just ONE POINT is often enough to win the game."

"Sam. You're good at maths. What's better, a ROOK or a BISHOP and a KNIGHT?"

"The ROOK is 5 points. The BISHOP and the KNIGHT are both 3 points. 3 + 3 = 6 so BISHOP and KNIGHT are better."

"Well done. What about a BISHOP or TWO PAWNS?"

"A BISHOP is 3 points, and TWO PAWNS are 2 points. So a BISHOP is better."

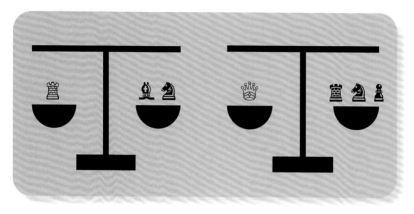

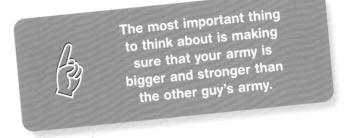

The most important thing to think about is making sure that your army is bigger and stronger than the other guy's army.

"Correct. Would you rather have a QUEEN, or a ROOK, a KNIGHT and a PAWN?"

"That's difficult. A ROOK is 5, a KNIGHT is 3 and a PAWN is 1. That makes 9 points which is the same as a QUEEN. So they're the same?"

"Right again. I can tell you're good at maths. Now listen carefully, both of you.

When you play your first games you'll find it very hard to see everything that's going on. The battlefield is a very big place and there's always a lot happening. So in every game you'll make lots of moves that lose points. If you want to be good enough to take on the Caïssan army you have to avoid making mistakes. It takes a few years for most kids to learn how to do this. But there is one way to learn more quickly."

"What's that?" asked Sam.

"It's very simple. I want you to play some games against FISHY and KASPY. If you look on the right of your screen you'll find the moves of the game, using the names of the squares. When you've finished the game press the PRINT GAME button and bring the moves in to show me. Every time you make a move that loses points you have to pay me. £100 for every point you lose. So if you lose a QUEEN for

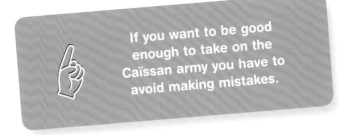

If you want to be good enough to take on the Caïssan army you have to avoid making mistakes.

nothing you have to pay me £900 because the QUEEN is worth 9 points. If you lose a QUEEN but get a ROOK in return you make a loss of four points – that's 9 take away 5 – so you have to pay me £400."

"That's so unfair!" exclaimed Sam. "You can't do that! We haven't got that much money."

"Listen, Sam," said Alice. "I've got a great idea. We could try it when we play Dad. He's really stupid so he'll lose all his pieces!"

"Yes," added Sam. "Just think how much money he'll have to pay us! We're sure to make a profit."

"What happens if you lose your KING?" asked Alice.

"Good question. Your money or your life. If you make a mistake and get CHECKMATED you get your head chopped off!

"Oh, and by the way. Don't forget that the threat is stronger than the execution."

CHAPTER 12
FOOL'S MATE

Game 1: Sam is the WHITE KING, Alice is the BLACK QUEEN.

I T WAS SAM'S FIRST battle as a KING. "Well, I could move any of the PAWNS," he thought to himself. "They all look much the same to me." So, choosing a pawn at random, he ordered the soldier on f2 to advance one square. In reply, the black pawn on e7 moved two squares to e5.

The white pawns still all looked the same so Sam, tossing an eight-sided coin, sent his g-pawn forward two squares to g4. The black king ordered Alice to move all the way along the diagonal, from d8 to h4. "CHECK!" he announced as Alice reached her destination.

"No problem," said Sam. "I can move somewhere safe to get out of check." The only square seemed to be f2 so he set off in that direction.

"You can't do that," said Alice. I'll still be checking you there. Maybe you can block the check instead."

"Or, better still, maybe one of my pieces can take you," said Sam. He looked round, asked the other pieces, but it seemed like Alice was safe from capture. "Never mind, I'll have to do what you said and put something in the way." He looked at each piece in turn but it seemed that none of them could move to block the check.

"It's CHECKMATE, I'm afraid, Sam. You're dead."

"I'm sorry, Sam," said Alice. "I didn't mean to kill, sorry, checkmate you. If I'd known it was CHECKMATE I'd have done something else instead."

"Don't be sorry, Alice. He may be your brother but in this battle he was the enemy, so you had to kill him. That's what happens in wars, remember. Oh, and, Sam, you get killed twice. You made the mistake that got yourself CHECKMATED so you get your head chopped off!"

"I couldn't help it," protested Sam. "It wasn't my fault."

"If you're the king it's always your fault, Sam. You're the one who makes the decisions. It was hard for you, though. There's a lot you have to learn before you'll be able to make good decisions.

"But you actually did something very clever, Sam. You found the quickest way to get CHECKMATED, in just two moves. It's called FOOL'S MATE. Anyone can make a mistake once, though. Only a fool makes the same mistake twice."

"How could I have stopped it?" asked Sam.

"First of all, it's very dangerous to move the pawns on the f-, g- and h-files at the start of the game. Moving those pawns can easily weaken your defences. The second piece of advice is to start in the middle of the board. If you do what the black army did and start by moving your e-pawn two squares you open up paths for your queen and bishop to move into the attack. I've told you that before: you must have forgotten.

"When both players have moved their e-pawns two squares, you can try moving your queen out to h5 as I

It's very dangerous to move the pawns on the f-, g- and h-files at the start of the game. Moving those pawns can easily weaken your defences.

suggested you did against FISHY and KASPY. But when you're playing against the complete army, it's dangerous – for both sides. Most strong players prefer to move their knight out to f3 to THREATEN the black pawn. Black usually DEFENDS the pawn by moving his knight to c6. Then you have a choice. Now the best ways to start games have been studied, sometimes for hundreds of years, and have been given names. Would you like to have a look at a few of them now?"

"Yes please," said Alice. "We could try to remember the moves and their names."

"Number one: White could bring the other knight out, to c3, when Black usually brings his other knight out to f6. This is called the FOUR KNIGHTS GAME.

"Number two: White could bring his bishop out from f1 to b5 to ATTACK the black knight. This is called the RUY LOPEZ or the SPANISH GAME."

"Ruy what?" asked Sam.

"RUY LOPEZ. He was a sixteenth century Spanish priest. Moving on to numbers three and four, White could also move his bishop to c4, to ATTACK the black pawn on f7. Then if Black plays knight to f6 it's the TWO KNIGHTS' DEFENCE and if he plays bishop to c5 instead, it's the GIUOCO PIANO or ITALIAN GAME."

"Giuoco who?" asked Sam.

"GIUOCO PIANO. It means QUIET GAME in Italian. Finally, number 5. White could move his pawn from d2 to d4 to challenge Black in the centre. This is the SCOTCH GAME. Do you think you could remember these moves and the names that go with them?"

"We'll try," said Alice. "Perhaps it would help if we practise them in our games as well."

"Good idea. And before you go, Sam, I'd like you to put your head on that block. Now be a good boy and don't move while I go and find my axe!"

CHAPTER 13

WATCHING THE ENEMY

Game 2: Sam is the WHITE KING, Alice is the WHITE QUEEN.

T HIS TIME SAM AND Alice were both in the white army. Sam tried to remember what he'd been told in the last lesson. Move your e-pawn, the one in front of the king. Then you can bring your queen and bishop into the attack. So he ordered the pawn right in front of him to move forward two squares. The black e-pawn also moved two squares, to e5, so now neither e-pawn could move. What next? Send Alice out to h5? It worked well for the black army in the last battle, and it also worked well against Fishy and Kaspy. So Alice moved to h5, on the side of the board. The black pawn on g7 now moved one square, to g6. Without looking or thinking, Sam instructed the bishop standing next to him to travel to c4.

The black soldier on g6 took out his sword...

"Help!!" screamed Alice. "I'm in danger from that pawn. I've got to move somewhere safe or I'll be killed!"

But it was too late. Sam didn't hear her and didn't see the danger. The black soldier on g6 took out his sword and Alice fell to the ground.

"I'm stopping the battle there, Sam, before you get anyone else killed. It's a win for the black army. And, Sam, you have to pay me £900."

"It was all your fault," protested Sam. "You made me lose. I did what you told me to do. I moved the e-pawn, then brought out the queen and the bishop. How was I to know that pawn was going to kill Alice? You're the one who should have to pay me £900!"

"Calm down, Sam, and let's see what went wrong. Remind me. What do you do before you cross the road?"

"I stop, look and listen."

"And what happens if you don't?"

"I get killed!"

"It's exactly the same on the battlefield, Sam. You didn't stop. You didn't look at what the enemy was doing. And you didn't listen to Alice when she told you she was in danger. But this time it was Alice, not you, who got killed."

"I couldn't help it, though."

"No, Sam. You could help it. You have to learn to concentrate and watch your opponent's move. Look very carefully at the piece he's just moved and see if there is a THREAT."

"What do you mean by a THREAT?" asked Sam.

"A THREAT is a move that THREATENS to gain points. It can be an ATTACK on an undefended piece. Or it can be an ATTACK by a weaker piece on a stronger piece. So if a pawn ATTACKS anything other than a pawn it's a THREAT. If a bishop or knight ATTACKS a rook or a queen it's a THREAT. And if a rook ATTACKS a queen it's a THREAT. But a QUEEN can only THREATEN an UNDEFENDED piece."

You have to learn to concentrate and watch your opponent's move. Look very carefully at the piece he's just moved and see if there is a THREAT.

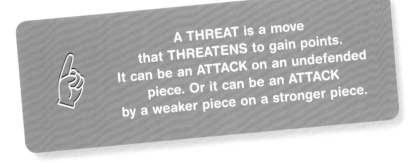

A THREAT is a move that THREATENS to gain points. It can be an ATTACK on an undefended piece. Or it can be an ATTACK by a weaker piece on a stronger piece.

"I don't quite understand about UNDEFENDED PIECES," said Sam.

"OK. Watch this. White moves his pawn from e2 to e4 and Black moves his pawn from e7 to e5. Just like your game started. Now suppose White moves his knight from g1 to f3. This move ATTACKS the black pawn on e5. In other

words, White could capture it next move. Black would not be able to take back because the pawn on e5 is UNDEFENDED. This means that White is THREATENING the pawn. So Black might reply by moving his knight from b8 to c6. This move DEFENDS the THREATENED pawn on e5. Now White COULD capture the pawn on e5 with his knight, but Black, in turn, would capture the white knight with his knight on c6. White would win ONE POINT but would lose THREE POINTS in return – not a good deal."

"I think I understand so far," said Alice.

"Now suppose White moves the bishop on f1 to b5, ATTACKING the knight on c6, which is DEFENDED by the pawns on b7 and d7. The bishop and the knight are both

worth THREE POINTS so that would be a fair exchange. Black can now THREATEN the bishop on b5 by moving his pawn from a7 to a6.

"I get it now," said Sam. "I always have to look at my opponent's last move. If he's trying to WIN POINTS by attacking a stronger piece or an undefended piece then I have to do something about it."

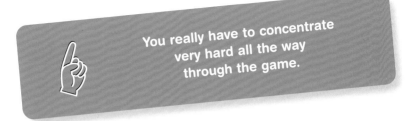

You really have to concentrate very hard all the way through the game.

"That's right, Sam. And to do that you really have to concentrate very hard all the way through the game. You have to look at the board all the time. If you don't see your opponent's move you won't be able to look at what he's THREATENING. It's hard enough when you're playing a human opponent, but it's very easy not to notice when you're playing a computer. If you're playing against FISHY or KASPY you can look at the scoresheet on the right of the screen and it will tell you their last move. But it's much better if you can train yourself to concentrate all the time. Try to clear all the other junk out of your head and focus only on what you're doing at the time. If you can learn to do this you'll do better at school as well."

Try to clear all the other junk out of your head and focus only on what you're doing at the time. If you can learn to do this you'll do better at school as well.

"Is there anything else I can do to concentrate better?" asked Sam.

"Next lesson, bring in the scoresheets from your games against FISHY and KASPY. We'll go through them together and see how many times you lost a piece because you didn't see your opponent's THREAT. Fining you doesn't seem to have helped your concentration so we'll try something different. I'll have to whack you once with a big stick for every point you lose in this way. If you don't want to get whacked you'll have to concentrate REALLY hard. There are also some concentration tests on our website. Spend some time on these every day and you'll find your concentration improving."

CHAPTER 14

LOOKING FOR CAPTURES

Game 3: Sam is the WHITE KING, Alice is the WHITE QUEEN.

O NCE AGAIN, SAM and Alice were both in the white army. The battle started the same way as last time. Sam ordered his e-pawn to move to e4 and the black king sent his e-pawn to e5. Again, Sam instructed Alice to travel to h5. And again the black g-pawn moved to g6. "It worked last time," thought the black king. "Perhaps it will work again."

"I'm in danger again, Sam," shouted Alice.

This time Sam stopped, looked and listened. "You'd better move, Alice. What do you want to do?"

Alice looked round. "I could capture the pawn on e5, I suppose. I think that would be check as well. Do you want me to do that?"

"Yes, if you want," replied Sam.

"CHECK!" Alice shouted, as her sword pierced the enemy soldier on e5. In reply, the black bishop on f8 moved to e7, BLOCKING the CHECK.

Alice looked again. "I can kill the rook on h8 now, I think."

"Good idea," said Sam. "Go ahead!"

Alice moved to h8, and the black rook fell to the ground. The black knight on b8 now moved to c6.

"Kill the knight on g8, Alice," yelled Sam. Alice did as she was told.

"Right, I'm going to stop the battle there. I've never seen so much carnage. It's a win for the white army. Well played, Sam and Alice."

"I'm not sure about killing all those soldiers," said Alice. "Are you sure they'll be all right?"

"Yes, don't worry about them. They were only slightly killed, not seriously killed. They'll recover in time for the next battle."

"It's not fair," complained Sam. "Why does Alice get to do all the killing? Why can't I kill anyone?"

"You chose to train to be the king, Sam. You can still change your mind and train to be a queen if you want."

"No way!" replied Sam. "Only girls can become queens. But I still don't think it's fair."

"Anyway, you both learnt a very important lesson today. Always look for captures. Every move. Every game. Don't forget. It's your job, Sam, to look at every one of the pieces in your army – all sixteen of them – and see what they can capture. If you can capture an UNDEFENDED PIECE – remember what they are? – then it's usually right to do so."

"What if the piece is defended?" asked Alice.

"Then it depends which piece is more valuable. If you can take a more valuable piece with a less valuable piece then you should usually do so. Even if you get taken back you'll still make a profit. So if one of your pawns could take a knight, bishop, rook or queen you should usually do so. If a bishop or knight could take a rook or a queen, again, you

Always look for captures.
Every move. Every game.
Don't forget.

should probably do it. And if a rook can take a queen, it will be worth it. Don't worry about losing one of your pieces if you can gain a more valuable piece in return."

"What about taking a piece of equal value?" asked Sam.

"Then that would be a fair exchange. A pawn for a pawn, a knight or bishop for a knight or bishop, a rook for a rook or a queen for a queen. They are all equal exchanges. Should you make an equal exchange? It all depends.

"If your army is stronger than the enemy army it's usually a good idea to exchange queens, rooks, bishops or knights. Suppose you're playing FISHY or KASPY and he's giving you a start. Then you should try to trade off his best pieces. Then it will be safer for your other pieces to take his pawns and easier for you to get CHECKMATE. Look at it this way. An army of 100 men is only a bit stronger than an army of 99 men but an army of two men is twice as strong as an army of one man.

"Bring in the games you play against FISHY and KASPY before the next lesson and we'll look at where you had a chance to win a piece."

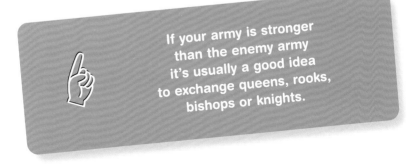

If your army is stronger than the enemy army it's usually a good idea to exchange queens, rooks, bishops or knights.

"Do we get £100 for every point we win?" asked Sam.

"No, I'm afraid not. You get whacked with a big stick for every point you could have won but didn't notice. And remember, Sam. Whatever doesn't kill you makes you stronger!"

CHAPTER 15

SAFETY FIRST

Game 4: Sam is the BLACK KING, Alice is the BLACK QUEEN.

THIS TIME, SAM AND Alice were in the black army. The white e-pawn advanced two squares, from e2 to e4, and Sam sent the black e-pawn forward from e7 to e5, leaving the two pawns blocked in the centre. Now the white knight moved out from g1 to f3.

Sam remembered what he'd been told and stopped to look at the knight. It was attacking the pawn on e5, he noticed. "But who cares about pawns?" thought Sam. "They're only worth one point. Last time I sent Alice out and she slaughtered most of the enemy army. I'll do the same thing again."

So Sam sent Alice out along the diagonal to the h4 square. As soon as she arrived there the horse on f3 leapt to

The white knight drew his lance...

h4. Its rider drew his lance and pierced Alice through the heart.

"I'm sorry, Alice," apologised Sam. "I didn't mean to... I mean... I wasn't concentrating. I didn't look first. I don't know what happened."

"It's another important lesson for you, Sam. It's also one of the hardest lessons to learn in chess. When you've thought of a move, it's very easy to play it without checking it through. But instead you must ask yourself if the move is safe. If you move that piece to that square will your opponent be able to capture it safely? There are two reasons why this is a hard lesson to learn. Firstly, when you've come up with what you think is a good move you get so excited

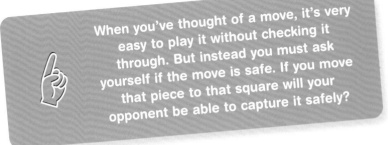

When you've thought of a move, it's very easy to play it without checking it through. But instead you must ask yourself if the move is safe. If you move that piece to that square will your opponent be able to capture it safely?

that it's hard to resist the temptation to play it at once. Secondly, you have to see something that's not on the board in front of you."

"So what should we do instead if they bring their knight to f3?" asked Alice, who had by now recovered.

"What do you think, Alice?"

"Well, he's ATTACKING our pawn on e5 so maybe we should DEFEND it. Earlier you told us to DEFEND by moving the knight on b8 to c6. Don't you remember, Sam?"

"Good thinking, Alice. Even one pawn is important in chess, because that extra pawn might one day become a queen. Don't think for a moment that pawns aren't important. There are several ways to DEFEND the pawn but the best, as I told you before, is to move your knight from b8 to c6.

Even one pawn is important in chess, because that extra pawn might one day become a queen.

"Let me tell you some more about knights. Take an empty chessboard and put a knight on f3. Do you remember how many squares it can move to from there?"

"Eight, isn't it?" replied Sam.

"That's right. And how many squares can it move to from h3?"

"Let me count – I think it's four," replied Sam again.

"Correct. So the knight is twice as good on f3 as on h3. Knights are good pieces to bring out early in the game because they can jump over everything in their way. And,

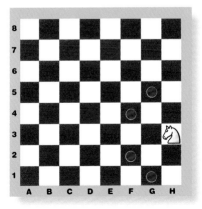

because they like to be in the middle, the white knights often go to f3 and c3, and the black knights to f6 and c6."

"So that's why the best way to defend the pawn is for the knight to move to c6," said Alice.

"Very good. That's one reason anyway. But now we have to sort Sam out. How do we get you to remember to check your move is safe before playing it?"

"Do I get whacked nine times?" asked Sam.

"Whacking you doesn't seem to work, does it? No. This time I want you to do 900 lines. That's 100 for every point you lost. 'I MUST REMEMBER TO CHECK THAT MY MOVE IS SAFE BEFORE PLAYING IT'. Bring it in for me next week."

"Why are you always so mean to me?" asked Sam.

"You have to learn how not to make mistakes if you want to beat the Caïssans."

"How long will that take?" asked Sam.

"Listen, Sam. Chess is a really hard game. Even the best players in the world make mistakes. And the best way to improve is to understand your mistakes and learn from them."

"What do you think, Sam?" said Alice. "When Dad loses his queen, should we fine him £900, whack him nine times or make him write 900 lines?"

"I think we should do all three," replied Sam. "Otherwise he'll never learn."

Chess is a really hard game. Even the best players in the world make mistakes. And the best way to improve is to understand your mistakes and learn from them.

CHAPTER 16

THE GUILLOTINE

"WHY IS YOUR ARM in a sling, Sam?"

"My hand hurts so much from writing all those lines. The doctor says I can't use it for two weeks."

"Why didn't you use a computer instead? Cut and paste. Much quicker and easier."

"Oh. I didn't think of that."

"It's the same in chess, Sam. The first move you think of might not be the best. And that was what happened last week, wasn't it?"

"He's joking, you know," said Alice. "What really happened was he fell off his bike. That's why he hasn't done the lines."

"Anyway, this week we're going to look at some CHECKMATES. Sam, as the king, you need to know all about CHECKMATES so you know what to avoid. And, Alice, the queen is the piece that most often gives CHECKMATE so you need lots of practice in doing CHECKMATES."

"How many different CHECKMATES are there?" asked Alice.

"Thousands. Probably millions. But there are two sorts of CHECKMATE which happen very often. The one we're going to look at today is the GUILLOTINE.

"Now, Sam. I want you to put your head on that block over there. When Alice presses the button the blade will come down and chop your head off."

" Now, Sam. I want you to put your head
on that block over there."

Sam wasn't very happy about this. "There's no way I'm going to do that! I don't want my head chopped off!"

"Don't worry, Sam. You can get a new one at the hospital. They do very good artificial heads these days. Your mum will hardly notice the difference."

"You need a new head, you know," added Alice. "The one you've got at the moment isn't much good. And it will go well with your new arm!"

"Don't talk to me like that, Alice," shouted Sam. "If my arm wasn't in a sling I'd knock your head off!"

"Now now, kids. Stop arguing and listen to me. You've seen something like this before but I'll show you again. Sam, you're the black king. Go and stand on g8. Alice, you're the white queen on d1, and I'm a white rook on a7. Now, Alice, you move right up the battlefield from d1 to d8. What can you do, Sam?"

"I can't move sideways because Alice will get me. And if I try to move up the board you'll get me. I'm in CHECK as well, so it's CHECKMATE."

"That's right. The GUILLOTINE is a CHECKMATE where the king is on the edge of the board, and a queen or a rook comes down to CHECK him along the side. Sometimes it's CHECKMATE because there's another piece stopping him escaping, like the rook here.

"Now, Alice, move back to d1 while I get three black pawns to stand on f7, g7 and h7. You don't need my help this time. Run up the battlefield again, just like the

The GUILLOTINE is a CHECKMATE where the king is on the edge of the board, and a queen or a rook comes down to CHECK him along the side.

GUILLOTINE blade coming down on Sam's neck. Don't forget to shout 'CHECKMATE' when you get there. Why can't you escape this time, Sam?"

"Because the pawns are in the way," answered Sam.

"Right again. There are also positions where some squares are blocked by your pawns and other squares are attacked by enemy pieces. Have a look at these positions and see if you can work out why they are all CHECKMATE."

"Can any other pieces do the GUILLOTINE?" asked Alice.

"You're an intelligent girl. What do you think?"

"The rook can, can't it? The knight can't and the bishop can't. And the pawn certainly can't."

"Next time try to answer your own question before you ask me. You can't ask any questions when you're playing chess, you know. Anything else?"

"Yes," said Sam. "What's the best way to stop the GUILLOTINE?"

"Good question, Sam. First of all, if you're on g1 or g8 because you've CASTLED on the king side, try to keep a rook nearby, on f1 or e1 for instance. If you can't do that it's a good idea to move up one of the pawns in front of you so that you have an escape square."

"We need to remember that CHECKMATE," said Sam. "Then we can use it next time we play Dad."

"You can also use it next time you play FISHY or KASPY. If they have their king on the edge of the board, put your queen on the next row to stop him escaping: like this. See

how the white queen traps the black king on the BACK RANK. All White has to do is move his pawn to the end of the board and PROMOTE it to a QUEEN or a ROOK and it's CHECKMATE. If you win some games like this, print off the moves and bring them in to show me."

If they have their king on the edge of the board, put your queen on the next row to stop him escaping.

CHAPTER 17
THE KISS OF DEATH

"LAST TIME YOU LEARNT about the GUILLOTINE. This time I want to show you a different sort of CHECKMATE.

"Sam. You're the black king again so go and stand on e8. Alice, you're the white queen. I want you to go and stand next to Sam on e7."

"I can kill her there, can't I?" asked Sam.

"You could if your arm wasn't in a sling, yes. But here I'm the white king and I'm going to stand on e6. What's happening now, do you think?"

"He can't kill me now," said Alice. "You can't have two kings standing together. So I think it's CHECKMATE."

"Indeed it is, Alice. This CHECKMATE is called the KISS OF DEATH. What happens now is that you have to kiss the black king. It's a poisoned kiss so the king will die."

"There's no way she's going to kiss me," protested Sam. "I'd rather have my head chopped off with the GUILLOTINE than have Alice kiss me."

"I'm not going to kiss him either. He's such an ugly frog," said Alice.

"Then if you kiss him he'll turn into a handsome prince. Or a handsome king."

"How dare you call me ugly!" yelled Sam. "Just you wait till my hand's better!"

"That's enough, both of you. If you're not careful, Sam, you'll have both arms in a sling by the time I've finished with you!

"Now pay attention to the lesson. Yes, Alice, you're right. It's CHECKMATE. In the KISS OF DEATH the enemy king is on the side of the board. Your queen, which is DEFENDED by another piece, is on the next square away from the side. It would still be CHECKMATE if I was on d6 or f6 instead. It doesn't have to be the king holding the queen's hand, though. It could be a rook, a bishop, a knight, a pawn or even another queen. Just as long as the queen is

In the KISS OF DEATH the enemy king is on the side of the board. Your queen, which is DEFENDED by another piece, is on the next square away from the side.

defended and cannot be taken by another piece it will be CHECKMATE.

"Now, Alice, I want you to move to f7. Is it CHECKMATE now, Sam?"

Sam looked around. "I can move to d8, I think."

"Yes, you can. But if there was a black queen on d8 then it would be CHECKMATE again. And that's another sort of KISS OF DEATH."

"Can any other piece do the KISS OF DEATH?" asked Alice.

"It's nearly always the queen that does the KISS OF DEATH, so you need to know it really well. And Sam, you need to know it as well. If you see the enemy queen heading for a square in front of you, make sure it's well defended.

"At the end of the game, when your opponent doesn't have many pieces left, you will often be able to get CHECKMATE using the KISS OF DEATH. And if you don't have a queen you can try to get a pawn to the end of the board and PROMOTE it to a queen. But you can use the KISS OF DEATH at any time in the game.

"Here's the starting position. There you are, Sam, the black king on e8. The d7 square is DEFENDED by a knight, a bishop, and the queen. The e7 square is also DEFENDED by a knight, a bishop and the queen. Which other pieces are DEFENDING the f7 square, Sam?"

"I can't see any at all."

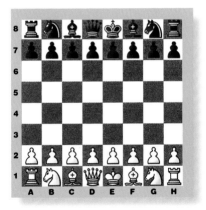

"Yes, you are the only piece DEFENDING f7. So sometimes you can get a quick attack at the start of the game by going for the f7 square. See if you can work out for yourself which pieces you can use to do this."

"Wicked!" said Sam. "We'll try it out when we play Dad tonight."

"Before you go, I'm going to give you both a worksheet with puzzles where you have to find the CHECKMATE. All of them will be either the GUILLOTINE or the KISS OF DEATH. And if that's too easy for you there are also some worksheets with all sorts of CHECKMATES on them. See how many CHECKMATE worksheets you can complete by next week. The more you can do the better I'll like it!"

"Perhaps Dad could help us," suggested Alice.

"No way. He's too stupid. They'll be much too hard for him," replied Sam.

CHAPTER 18

SCHOLAR'S MATE

Game 5: Sam is the WHITE KING, Alice is the WHITE QUEEN.

"WHAT'S THAT CAMERA doing up there?" asked Sam. "Is it to film the battles?"

"That's one reason, yes. It's always a good idea to go through your battles again so that you can learn from your mistakes. But there's also another reason. The camera is a CCTV – a Close Circuit TeleVision. But CCTV stands for something else as well.

"The first C stands for CHECKS. Always look at every CHECK because it might be CHECKMATE.

"The second C stands for CAPTURES. Always look to see if you can make a CAPTURE that wins points – by taking an UNDEFENDED piece or a stronger piece.

"The T stands for THREATS. Can I THREATEN one of his pieces? Is he THREATENING one of my pieces?

CHECKS, CAPTURES and THREATS are the three sorts of move you always have to look for.

"CHECKS, CAPTURES and THREATS are the three sorts of move you always have to look for."

"What does the V stand for?" asked Sam.

"The V stands for VIOLENCE, which is what I do to you if you get it wrong! It also stands for VICTORY, which is what happens if you get it right!"

"Cool," said Sam. "Let's try it out in a battle. We're White this time, then?"

Sam sent his e-pawn up to e4, and the black e-pawn moved to e5. Sam ordered Alice up the diagonal to h5, and this time the black knight on b8 moved to c6.

"Look, Alice," said Sam. "There are three pawns you could CAPTURE. Two of them are CHECKS as well. Which one do you want to do?"

"I don't think they're safe, Sam," Alice replied. "If I take on e5, the knight will take me. If I take on f7, the king will take me. And if I take on h7, the rook will take me. Ask the other pieces what they want to do."

"Remember about getting a quick attack on f7," said Sam. "Perhaps the bishop on f1 could move to c4."

So Sam sent his bishop to c4, and the black army replied by moving their knight from g8 to f6.

Sam and Alice both looked at their enemy's move closely. "I'm under attack!" exclaimed Alice. "I need to find a safe square."

"Remember the CCTV," said Sam. "Can you play any CHECKS or CAPTURES?"

"I could still take on e5, but it's defended by the knight on c6. Wait a minute. I think it's safe to take on f7 now. The king wouldn't be able to take me because of the bishop on c4."

"I could take the pawn on f7 as well," interrupted the bishop on c4. "Alice is worth more than me. She might be in danger. I think it would be safer if I captured the pawn."

"But I could do more damage because I'm more powerful," exclaimed Alice. "I think I should take the pawn."

Sam was confused. "I don't know what to do. What do you think?"

"You're the king, Sam. Only you can make the decision. There are two possible moves. Which one do you think is best? Think about it!"

Sam stopped to think. "Just a minute! It's the KISS OF DEATH, isn't it? I think it's CHECKMATE if Alice takes the pawn on f7. The king can't take Alice because the bishop on c4 is holding her hand. He can't move anywhere else. And I don't think anyone else can take her."

So Alice took the pawn on f7, and, at the same time, kissed the black king. Her sword killed the pawn and her kiss killed the king.

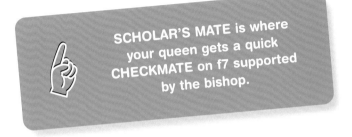

SCHOLAR'S MATE is where your queen gets a quick CHECKMATE on f7 supported by the bishop.

Alice's sword killed the pawn and her kiss killed the king.

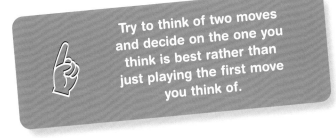

Try to think of two moves and decide on the one you think is best rather than just playing the first move you think of.

"Congratulations, kids! You got CHECKMATE in just four moves. This is called SCHOLAR'S MATE. SCHOLAR'S MATE is where your queen gets a quick CHECKMATE on f7 supported by the bishop. Everyone learning chess has to know this one.

"One other thing. We have to make decisions every move. Try to think of two moves and decide on the one you think is best rather than just playing the first move you think of."

"We could try SCHOLAR'S MATE on Dad, couldn't we?" suggested Alice. "I think he'll probably fall for it."

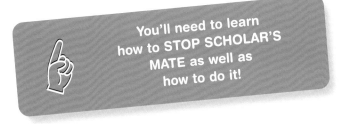

You'll need to learn how to STOP SCHOLAR'S MATE as well as how to do it!

"You could well be right, but then he might learn it and try it out on you. In which case you'll need to learn how to STOP SCHOLAR'S MATE as well as how to do it! Moving the knight to f6 was a big mistake: the black king didn't look at your THREAT. Try to think which moves Black could have played to DEFEND f7 again, or to BLOCK one of your attacking pieces. If you need any help there's a lesson on our website to help you. After all, you might need to know this yourself when you come to battle the Caïssans."

CHAPTER 19

THE QUEEN FORK

Game 6: Sam is the BLACK KING, Alice is the BLACK QUEEN.

" I 'VE GOT A NEW WEAPON for you, Alice. It's called a FORK. If you THREATEN one enemy soldier he can defend himself or run away. You can use a FORK to THREATEN two enemy soldiers at the same time. Then, when one of them defends himself you might be able to kill the other one next move!"

"Awesome!" exclaimed Sam. "Can I have one too?"

"Yes, Sam. All the soldiers in the army can use FORKS. But your job is to stay safe while making decisions, so you won't need to use your FORK very often.

"Anyway, let's see if Alice can use her FORK in your next battle."

Again, the white army started by moving the pawn from e2 to e4. This time Sam decided to try something different.

> You can use a FORK to THREATEN two enemy soldiers at the same time. Then, when one of them defends himself you might be able to kill the other one next move!

He told his c-pawn to go from c7 to c5. This would give Alice the chance to move out and perhaps use her FORK.

Now the white pawn on d2 went to d4. Sam was watching carefully. "Interesting," he thought. "He's trying to take our guy on c5, but we can take him first." So he ordered the black pawn on c5 to capture the white pawn on d4. Now, instead of taking the pawn back with their queen, the white army moved their knight from g1 to f3.

Sam again stopped to think. He looked at the knight and saw that he was THREATENING the pawn on d4. He could get the e-pawn to defend his friend by moving to e5.

The white knight moved again, jumping to the e5 square and capturing the black footsoldier.

"Oh no!" exclaimed Sam. "I hadn't seen that. I'd forgotten to check if the move was safe. Now I'm going to be in trouble again."

"Hold on!" shouted Alice. "I've got my FORK here. Perhaps I can use it."

"Don't forget to look for CHECKS, CAPTURES and THREATS," Sam reminded her.

"I can move to a5," said Alice. "That's CHECK. And look! It's THREATENING the white knight on e5 as well. I'm using my FORK to THREATEN two enemy pieces at the same time. I don't think the knight on e5 can BLOCK the check either."

"Well played, Alice! You used your FORK to win the white knight. And well done too, Sam. You set a very clever trap there!"

"A trap? I didn't know I'd set a trap. I didn't see they could take the pawn."

"In that case you were lucky as well as honest. You might not get away with forgetting to check that your move was safe next time.

"By the way, Alice, it's not the first time you've used a FORK. Here, take a look at this. Do you remember this game? You were White. The game started with White moving from e2 to e4 and Black moving from e7 to e5. You moved to h5 and the black pawn moved from g7 to g6."

"Yes, I think I remember. I captured the pawn on e5 next, didn't I?"

"Well remembered! This is also a QUEEN FORK. You were CHECKING the black king and also THREATENING the rook on h8. Black had to BLOCK the CHECK by putting a piece in the way, leaving you free to capture the rook next move."

"Do QUEEN FORKS happen a lot?" asked Alice.

"Yes, they do. But because they often happen at a long distance they're very easy to miss. The queen always has to look very carefully at every square just in case there's a chance for a FORK. Why do you think queens are so good at doing FORKS, Sam?"

"Is it because they're very powerful?"

Don't forget to look for CHECKS, CAPTURES and THREATS.

The queen always has to look very carefully at every square just in case there's a chance for a FORK. Knights are also very good at doing FORKS.

"Partly, yes. And also because they can move in eight directions, remember. Apart from kings and queens, what other pieces can move in eight directions?"

"A knight in the middle can move to eight squares," answered Sam. "Is that what you mean?"

"That's right. So knights are also very good at doing FORKS. The king has to make sure his queen and his knights know all about how to use FORKS. Here's another question for you. How can White win a bishop by playing a QUEEN FORK in the position shown below? Don't forget to look out for CHECKS!"

"It's easy," said Alice. "The white queen can go to h5. It's CHECK and it also THREATENS the black bishop on c5."

"Well done! If you look on our website you'll find a QUEEN FORK quiz to do at home. And remember to look out for them in your games against FISHY, KASPY and DEEP RED."

CHAPTER 20

THE KNIGHT FORK

Game 7: Sam is the BLACK KING, Alice is the BLACK QUEEN.

I N THE NEXT BATTLE, Sam and Alice were again in the black army. The white king sent his pawn forward from e2 to e4 and Sam asked his e-pawn to move from e7 to e5. The white knight on g1 went to f3 and, remembering what he'd been taught, Sam ordered his knight on b8 to go to c6 and DEFEND the e-pawn.

Next, the white bishop on f1 travelled to c4. Sam remembered to look at this move carefully. The bishop was

ATTACKING the black pawn on f7, but Sam himself was defending the pawn. What now? He knew it was a good idea to bring your knights into the centre at the start of the game, so he sent his other knight out from g8 to f6.

The white knight on f3 now moved again, to g5. Sam took a quick look. The knight was attacking the h7 pawn which was DEFENDED by a rook, and he was DEFENDING the pawn on f7. He decided it would be a good idea to THREATEN the knight and send him back again so he invited his pawn to move from h7 to h6.

Much to Sam's surprise, the knight on g5 didn't retreat, but instead captured the pawn on f7. Without thinking, Sam took out his sword and stabbed the soldier riding the horse. "Finally I get to kill someone!" he exclaimed.

"Not so fast," shouted the white bishop on c4. "I can kill you now. That means the white army wins the battle."

When an ILLEGAL MOVE is played you have to take the move back and play something else instead.

"I'm going to stop the battle there and explain a rule to you. First of all, Mr Bishop, you are not allowed to kill the black king. The black army made an ILLEGAL MOVE when the king moved into CHECK. The rule is that when an ILLEGAL MOVE is played you have to take the move back and play something else instead. So the white knight has to get back on his horse and return to f7 while the black king has to return to e8.

"Now, in a real battle Sam would have to move somewhere else himself – if you touch a piece deliberately you have to move it. But as it's only a practice battle I'll let you off. The black army has to make a different move, though. What are you going to do, Sam?"

"Help! I'm being attacked!" shouted Alice.

"Help! I'm being attacked!" shouted the rook on h8, who had the louder voice.

Sam, flustered by his mistake, only heard the rook, and commanded him to move to g8.

The white knight gleefully leapt to d8, knocking Alice over as he did so.

"I'm sorry," said Sam. "I wasn't concentrating. My teacher says that if I could concentrate better I'd be top of the class."

"No way!" said Alice. "You'll never be top of the class while I'm around. Besides, everyone knows that girls are smarter than boys."

"Leave it for now, Alice. Sam's having a bad day. If I knew how to help kids concentrate better I'd be rich. You really have to learn to switch off everything else in your head and focus only on what you are supposed to be doing."

"It was another attack on f7, wasn't it? But with a bishop and a knight instead of a bishop and a queen. I think I'd have seen it if I'd been concentrating."

"And I think it was a KNIGHT FORK as well," added Alice. "The knight was THREATENING me as well as the rook. It would have been better if I'd moved to e7 instead of the rook moving. I'll have to shout louder next time."

"Listen, Sam. When your enemy uses a FORK, he creates two THREATS. If you can't meet both threats at once you have to work out the most important threat.

"By the way, Alice, here's the position after the white knight moved to g5. What do you think would be the best move here?"

> You really have to learn to switch off everything else in your head and focus only on what you are supposed to be doing.

"If I moved to e7 I could DEFEND the pawn on f7."

"Yes, but work out what would happen. Suppose his bishop captures the pawn. Now, if you capture the bishop, the knight will capture you. Then Sam could capture the knight. So you win a bishop and a knight but lose a queen and a pawn. You're good at maths Sam, so tell me how much loss you'd make."

"3 + 3 is 6, and 9 + 1 is 10, so I'd lose four points."

When your enemy uses a FORK, he creates two THREATS. If you can't meet both threats at once you have to work out the most important threat.

"Yes, so Alice moving to e7 wouldn't be the best move. You don't have any good way to DEFEND f7, so perhaps you could BLOCK the bishop instead."

"I've got it now," said Alice. "I think we should have moved the pawn on d7 to d5."

"You're quite right, Alice. That's the only good way to DEFEND against White's THREAT."

"I suppose I get another 900 lines for losing my queen," said Sam.

"You could take back the knight, so it's only 600 lines. But don't forget to use your computer. And just to make sure you understand all about KNIGHT FORKS, what do you think White should do here?"

"I could play a check with my KNIGHT on c7," said Sam. "I think it's safe."

"And look," said Alice. "It's THREATENING the black queen and the rook on a8 as well. That must be a TRIPLE FORK! KNIGHT FORKS are really cool. Can we practise some more at home?"

"Certainly, Alice. If you look on the website you'll find a lot more about FORKS, including a KNIGHT FORK QUIZ. See if you can get all the questions right before the next lesson."

TOUCH AND MOVE

The Touch and Move rule, which is used in all tournaments, states that if you touch one of your pieces deliberately you have to move it, and if you touch an enemy piece deliberately you have to take it. If you want to adjust a piece on a square you can say "J'ADOUBE" (an old French word) or "ADJUST" BEFORE you touch the piece you wish to adjust. You CANNOT say "adjust" after touching a piece because you've changed your mind and don't want to move it.

CHAPTER 21

THE PIN

Game 8: Sam is the BLACK KING, Alice is the BLACK QUEEN.

S AM AND ALICE WERE again in the black army. The white
e-pawn again moved forward two squares. This time
Sam had an idea to try something different. He could
send his d-pawn to d5. True, he'd be captured by the white
pawn on e4 but then Alice would be able to get into the
game by capturing on d5.

So his d-pawn advanced two squares, and, sure enough,
was captured by the white e-pawn. Sam ordered his sister to
travel to d5 and capture the white pawn. Now the white
knight moved out from b1 to c3.

"That knight's THREATENING me," shouted Alice. "I've
got to move somewhere safe."

"Where do you want to move to?" asked Sam.

Time stood still while Alice considered her options. There were lots of squares she could move to. Some were safe, but some were not. She could move to e5 or e6, perhaps. Then it would be CHECK but White could block the check so there didn't seem much point. But there were so many other squares she could move to. It was like deciding which dress to wear for a party. She really couldn't make up her mind.

"Hurry up!" yelled Sam impatiently. "We haven't got all day."

"She's thinking, Sam. How are you going to find the best move unless you think about it first?"

"No she's not," answered Sam. "She can never make up her mind about anything."

"Well, how am I supposed to know what to do?" asked Alice. "You're the king: you decide!"

"I'll choose a random square, then. How about c6? Is that safe?"

"I can't get captured there. Is that what you want me to do?"

"Yes, go on then. Move to c6."

The white king also stopped to think. Finally, he told the bishop on f1 to move to b5.

"That bishop's THREATENING me," said Alice. "If I capture him, the knight on c3 will capture me. What should I do, Sam?"

"You'll have to move sideways, Alice. How about d6? I think that's safe."

"Stop right there!" shouted the white king as Alice prepared to move. "You can't do that, you know!"

"Why not?" asked Alice.

"What's the problem?" added Sam.

"Can't you see?" replied the white king. If you move away you'll be in CHECK from the bishop on b5. I'm afraid there's no way out. You're going to be captured next move."

"Sorry, Sam, but you've got Alice killed again. This is another weapon you need to learn about. The white bishop was using a PIN."

"A PIN?" exclaimed Sam. "How does that work?"

"A PIN is a situation in which one of your pieces is in line with a king, or another enemy target it wants to take, and there's an enemy piece blocking the attack. The piece that's in the way is PINNED. The only pieces that can use PINS are bishops, rooks and queens. For example, look at the position here. The PINNING piece is the white bishop on b5. The TARGET, Sam, is YOU, the black king on e8. The

PINNED piece – the piece in between the PINNING piece and the TARGET – is you, Alice, the black queen on c6."

"So I can't move off the diagonal because that would leave Sam in check," said Alice.

"That's right, and because you are more valuable than the bishop, and the bishop is defended by the knight, the white army will win a queen in exchange for a bishop.

"There are different types of PIN, though. Some, like this one, will win points. Some are just a nuisance, while others are completely harmless.

"You already know that the knights will often come out to c3 and f3, c6 and f6 at the start of the game. Well, sometimes the bishops come out to b5 and g5 for White, and to b4 and g4 for Black. Look at this position. All four

bishops are PINNED by knights. The knights on c3 and c6 CANNOT move because they would leave the king IN CHECK. The knights on f3 and f6 CAN move but if they do so they would leave their queen to be captured. And that, Sam, is a VERY easy mistake to make."

"So PINS can be good, then, even if they don't win a better piece?" said Alice.

"Yes, so it's often worth putting your bishops and rooks in line with enemy kings and queens. Oh, and, Sam, that's another 600 lines."

A PIN is a situation in which one of your pieces is in line with a king, or another enemy target it wants to take, and there's an enemy piece blocking the attack. The piece that's in the way is PINNED.

"I didn't do anything wrong," protested Sam.

"I know it was hard for you because you didn't know about PINS, but you still have to learn to look at any CHECK, CAPTURE or THREAT your opponent might make next."

"But it was Alice's fault. She should have seen it. And she took so long to think about it as well. She should do the 600 lines, not me."

"You're the king, Sam. You have to learn to take responsibility for your own decisions. But this time we'll make it 300 lines each. Before you go, let's see if you really understand PINS. How can White use a PIN to win the black queen in this position?"

Alice looked carefully at the position. "The enemy king and queen are both on the e-file. I think I can do a PIN if I move my ROOK from f1 to e1. Is that right?"

"Yes, Alice. That's right. But there's a lot more to learn about PINS. Have a look at some of the lessons and quizzes on our website before the next lesson. And that goes for you as well, Sam."

CHAPTER 22
THE AMBUSH

Game 9: Sam is the BLACK KING, Alice is the BLACK QUEEN.

"**G**REAT! WE'RE BLACK AGAIN," exclaimed Sam. "I've got a really good idea about how we can win. All we do is copy the white moves until they make a mistake. That way we can't lose. Let's try it out."

So the white pawn moved from e2 to e4, and Sam sent his black pawn from e7 to e5. The white knight on g1 moved to f3, so Sam did the same thing and invited the knight on g8 to go to f6.

Now the white knight on f3 captured the black pawn on e5. "No problem," said Sam. "We'll do the same thing." And the black knight on f6 captured the pawn on e4.

Next, the white queen moved from d1 to e2. Sam stopped and looked at this move. "He's THREATENING the knight on e4. I suppose I'd better ask him to move back somewhere safe." So Sam sent the black knight back to f6.

The white king thought for some time about what to do next. Eventually he asked the knight on e5 to move to c6.

Sam and Alice both looked surprised. "He's THREATENING me," said Alice. "Don't worry," said Sam. "The pawn on d7 can take him. Oh, so can the pawn on b7. And the knight on c6. Which one would be best?"

"CHECK!!" announced the white king.

"Check? What are you talking about?" said Sam. "He's attacking the queen, not the king."

"Don't you see?" said the white king. "You're in CHECK from the queen, not the knight. It's a DISCOVERED CHECK!"

"Oh! I see it now. I can't move anywhere so I have to BLOCK the check. Alice, as you're in danger you can BLOCK the check by moving to e7."

"That's no good!" said Alice. "The knight on c6 will take me there. What can we do? How can I save myself?"

"I'm sorry, Alice, but there's nothing you can do. It doesn't matter which piece BLOCKS the check. The knight will capture you next move, either on e7 or d8."

"I don't understand what happened," said Sam. "How could the queen check me when the knight moved?"

"As the white king said, it's DISCOVERED CHECK. When the knight moved away he opened up the e-file for the queen to CHECK you. At the same time he THREATENED Alice, so when you stopped to save yourself he could capture Alice next move.

"Like a PIN you have an attacking piece, a queen, rook or bishop, lined up against an enemy target. But this time there's another attacking piece – the white knight – in the way. So, like a FORK your enemy is THREATENING two targets at the same time, but with two different pieces. It's like an AMBUSH. The knight who was hiding behind the white queen jumps out to attack the black queen."

"That's so unfair," complained Sam. "I've never seen anything like that before. How was I to know?"

"You might have seen it coming, Sam, when you saw the white queen land on e2. But your idea of copying the white

The knight who was hiding behind the white queen jumped
out to attack the black queen.

army was really not very sensible. Think about it, Sam. If
they play a capture you may not be able to copy them. If
they play a check you certainly can't copy them."

"So was it a mistake to copy their second move?" asked
Alice.

"No. Moving the knight from g8 to f6 is fine. But when
they take the pawn on e5 it's best to move the d-pawn to d6
to drive the knight away before taking the pawn on e4.

"Remember what I said last lesson. It's often a good idea to
line up a bishop or rook against an enemy queen or king. If one
of THEIR pieces is in the way you have a PIN. If one of YOUR

pieces is in the way you can do a DISCOVERED ATTACK or a DISCOVERED CHECK. And that move could be a CAPTURE or a THREAT. Or both. It could even be another CHECK in which case you've done a DOUBLE CHECK. And the only way to get out of a DOUBLE CHECK is to move your king."

"It's too hard for me," complained Sam. "How am I supposed to know what my opponent's going to do next?"

"Yes, Sam, I know it's hard. Hard things are worth doing. Easy things aren't. What's that camera up there?"

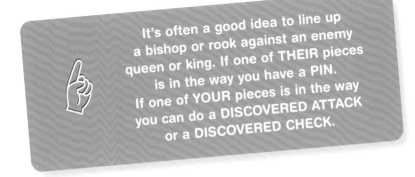

It's often a good idea to line up a bishop or rook against an enemy queen or king. If one of THEIR pieces is in the way you have a PIN. If one of YOUR pieces is in the way you can do a DISCOVERED ATTACK or a DISCOVERED CHECK.

Hard things are worth doing.
Easy things aren't.

"It's a CCTV."

"Yes – so you have to ask yourself: if I play that move what CHECKS, CAPTURES and THREATS does my opponent have? It needs a lot of practice to get used to doing it. Even the best players in the world sometimes get it wrong. But you still have another 600 lines to do though."

"I'm not going to do it. It's not my fault if you expect me to do things that are too hard for me. I'm quitting."

"Think about it, Sam, and tell me again next week. Meanwhile, Alice, have a look at this position. As Sam doesn't want to be the king any more, you're in command of

the black army. The white queen has just moved to g4, and, if you look, you'll see that she's on the same DIAGONAL as your BISHOP. What are you going to do about it?"

"I could move my pawn from d7 to d6," suggested Alice.

"You could – and they might not notice that you're THREATENING their queen. But you can do better, you know. What else could the pawn do?"

"It could move to d5, but it would be in danger there."

"Don't worry about that. If they take your pawn you'll take their queen. And if they move their queen you'll take their bishop. You have to learn to think about more than one thing at the same time when you play chess."

"Should I get some practice before the next lesson?"

"Yes, get on the internet and learn more about AMBUSHES while your brother's sitting around sulking. See you next lesson!"

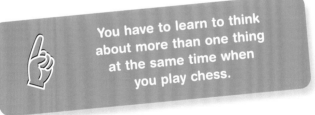

You have to learn to think about more than one thing at the same time when you play chess.

CHAPTER 23
THE FIRING SQUAD

"I'VE THOUGHT ABOUT IT," said Sam.

"And?"

"It's too hard for me. Every week I make a mistake and lose my queen. I can't help it. I'm giving up."

"You're being a coward, Sam."

"I don't care. I've made my mind up."

"In that case you give me no choice. Soldiers who refuse to fight in battles have to face the firing squad. Take the prisoner away."

Sam found himself in the middle of the battlefield, facing two rooks armed with rifles.

"You can't kill him," said Alice. "I know he's annoying but he's still my brother."

Sam found himself in the middle of the battlefield, facing two rooks armed with rifles.

"Don't worry, Alice. He'll be fine."

The rook on a1 moved to a5, opening fire on Sam. Sam jumped back to e4 to dodge the bullet, but the other rook moved from h1 to h4. BANG!! Another shot and again Sam escaped by moving to e3. The rook on a5 moved to a3, pulling the trigger as he did so. Sam ran back from e3 to e2, to be met by the other rook going from h4 to h2. There was nothing for it. Sam had to retreat to e1. The rook on a3 went to a1, setting his sights on his victim. BANG!! This time Sam had nowhere to go. Alice screamed as he fell to the ground in a pool of blood.

"That was fun!" said Sam. "I really like paintball, and that red paint looks just like blood! Can I try again, please? I think I've got a way to stop them."

"So you're not giving up after all? Excellent! If you really think you can survive next time go back to e5 and start again."

Sam returned to e5 and again the rook on a1 moved to a5. Sam was in CHECK and this time he went to f4. The other rook called CHECK as he went from h1 to h4, and Sam moved to g3, tackling the rook on h4 and trying to grab his rifle.

"What do you think the white army should do next, Alice?"

"Well, Sam's THREATENING the rook on h4. So he either has to defend himself or move away."

"So what would you do then?"

"I think I'd want to run as far away from Sam as possible."

"Good idea. Tell me what the rooks are doing."

"They're taking it in turns to shoot Sam. So I need to keep the rooks off the same file, don't I? In that case I'd move the rook from h4 to b4."

And, sure enough, the white rook on h4 moved to b4. Sam went to f3, trying to get back across to approach the rooks again, but he would be far too late.

The rook on a5 moved to a3. CHECK! Sam moved from f3 to e2. By now Sam knew what was coming next. The rook on b4 went to b2. CHECK! Sam tried going back to d1 but he was too slow. The rook on a3 moved to a1. CHECKMATE!!

"That CHECKMATE's the GUILLOTINE, isn't it?" said Alice.

"Yes, it is, but we call the plan to get CHECKMATE the FIRING SQUAD. The two rooks take it in turns to shoot the black king. Once he reaches the side of the board he has nowhere to run, nowhere to hide. One rook CHECKS while the other rook blocks his only escape route. Once you know it, it's very easy. If you happen to have a queen and a rook, or even two queens then it's even easier.

"Sometimes you get towards the end of the battle with a big advantage but it's not always easy to find a CHECKMATE. If you've got two rooks, or a rook and a queen on the board, try to use the FIRING SQUAD to finish off the game. If you just play random moves you might end up STALEMATING your opponent. You need a PLAN to finish off the battle, and the FIRING SQUAD is often the easiest plan to use to get an easy CHECKMATE."

"Oh, and Sam, don't ever think about quitting again. Quitting is for cowards. Heroes never give up. Are you a coward or a hero, Sam?"

"It's hard, though," said Sam. "Do I get any lines this week?"

"Not unless you really want them. Just go off and enjoy yourself. And practise the FIRING SQUAD as well."

"Are there any more CHECKMATES we could learn?" asked Sam.

The two rooks take it in turns to shoot the black king. Once he reaches the side of the board he has nowhere to run, nowhere to hide. One rook CHECKS while the other rook blocks his only escape route.

Quitting is for cowards. Heroes never give up.

"The two you'll need to learn are KING AND QUEEN against KING and KING AND ROOK against KING. In each case you have to use your two pieces together to force the enemy king to the edge of the board. With the KING and QUEEN you can use either the KISS OF DEATH or the GUILLOTINE to get CHECKMATE. With the KING AND ROOK you have to use the GUILLOTINE. Try them out for yourselves at home, or play them out against FISHY on our website."

CHAPTER 24

ALIEN INVASION

Game 10: Sam is the BLACK KING, Alice is the BLACK QUEEN.

"I'M AFRAID YOU LOST the toss, so you're in the black army again, kids. I don't know what's happened to the white army though. Stay there while I go and find them, and don't do anything stupid while I'm gone."

"This is boring, isn't it?" said Sam. "We've just got to stand around and wait for our opponents."

"Look over there, Sam!" exclaimed Alice. "There's a flying saucer. I think it's heading this way!"

"It's landing, Alice. Look, the aliens are getting out and coming over to us. This must be the Caïssan army. This is our big chance to become heroes, defeat the aliens and save the planet."

"I'm scared, Sam. They're the cruellest and most intelligent creatures in the universe and we're only kids. We don't stand a chance. They'll kill us and take over the planet."

"You should never give up, remember, Alice. If we remember everything we've been taught, concentrate really hard and try to think ahead then we stand a chance."

The Caïssan army took their places on the battlefield. "Ha!" said the Caïssan king in his strange alien language. "The earthlings are stupid. Their army is made up of kids. We'll win easily." He ordered his pawn to advance from e2 to e4.

"We know all about this move," said Sam, sending his pawn forward from e7 to e5. "Let's see which opening they're going to play."

If we remember everything we've been taught, concentrate really hard and try to think ahead then we stand a chance.

"We can win in four moves," said the Caïssan king. "Kids like that won't know about Scholar's Mate. Hey, Queen. Move from d1 to h5."

"We've seen this before as well, haven't we, Alice?" said Sam. "They're THREATENING the pawn on e5 so we should bring our knight from b8 to c6 to defend it."

So the black knight moved to c6 and the Caïssan army, following their plan, sent their bishop from f1 to c4.

"They're going for Scholar's Mate," said Sam. "How should we defend, Alice?"

"I could move to e7 or f6, I suppose, but it looks too scary. I'd much rather stay where I am. I really don't want them to kill me. Perhaps we should BLOCK the attack by moving the pawn on g7 to g6."

"Yes, good idea," said Sam, inviting the g-pawn to advance one square, THREATENING the enemy queen.

"They foiled our plan," said the Caïssan king. "They were lucky. We'll move the queen back to f3. They won't be lucky twice in a row."

"Don't forget to look at their move," said Alice. "What are they threatening?"

Sam looked at the enemy queen very carefully. "I think they're trying to get SCHOLAR'S MATE again. You could still move to e7 to DEFEND against the threat."

"It still might be too dangerous," said Alice. Ask the other pieces if they can help you."

The knight on g8 said that he could BLOCK the threat by moving to f6. That seemed like a good idea. Sam had been told it's a good idea to move your knights into the centre at the start of the game so he sent the knight into battle.

"They've stopped us again," said the Caïssan king. "How can we get that knight to move again? I know. If our pawn moves from g2 to g4, then next move he can go to g5, THREATENING the knight on f6. When it moves away,

It's a good idea to move your knights into the centre at the start of the game.

victory will be ours. We'll kill the feeble earthling army and take over the planet."

Sam was thinking really hard now. He'd never thought so hard in his life. Why did they play that move? Is it THREATENING anything? What are they planning to do next?

"They brought their queen out too soon. Perhaps we can attack her," suggested Alice.

Why did they play that move? Is it THREATENING anything? What are they planning to do next?

Sam looked at the CCTV watching the game. "Looking for CHECKS, CAPTURES and THREATS will lead to VICTORY. Can we THREATEN the alien queen? Can anyone help?"

The knight on c6 told Sam he could THREATEN the queen by moving to d4. Sam looked at that move and made sure it was safe, then ordered the knight to advance. "The knight's also THREATENING c2," said Alice. "If they move to e3 we can FORK their king, queen and rook!"

The Caïssan queen returned home to d1 to protect the pawn on c2, leaving Sam to consider the next move.

"What CHECKS, CAPTURES and THREATS do I have here?" asked Sam. "I think the knight on f6 could kill the pawn on e4 safely." He asked the knight, who agreed that it was a good idea.

The Caïssans were starting to get worried. The earthlings had made the first kill, and those two knights were looking very strong in the centre of the battlefield. In desperation, their king ordered the pawn on f2 to move to f3.

If you find a good move
you should look
for a better one.

Sam saw at once that the knight on e4 was in danger. "Where do you want to move to?" he asked him.

"Wait a minute," said Alice. "You haven't looked at all CHECKS, CAPTURES and THREATS yet. If you find a good move you should look for a better one."

"Yes," replied Sam. "I must try to think before deciding on my move. Hey, Alice. You could move to h4. That would be CHECK."

"I'm too scared to move," said Alice.

"You have to THINK AHEAD, Alice. Remember. Now if you moved to h4 would it be safe?"

"Well I wouldn't get taken there if that's what you mean."

"Right. Can they BLOCK the check? I don't think so. So they'd have to move the king. Let's see where he could move to. Interesting! He'd have to move to f1. Then what could we do?"

You must try to think before
deciding on your move.
You have to THINK AHEAD

"I could play a CHECK on h3," said Alice. "But that wouldn't be safe because of the knight on g1. Or I could CHECK on f2 but then the king would kill me. No, wait a minute, I'd be DEFENDED by the knight on e4."

"Alice!! It's the KISS OF DEATH, isn't it? He won't be able to kill you because the knight is holding your hand. And no one else can kill you either. Move to h4 and check him.

Alice was really frightened but she knew that the future of the planet was at stake. Moving to h4 was the bravest thing she'd ever done in her life. The Caïssan king had no choice. He had to move to f1.

"Do it, Alice," yelled Sam. "Move to f2 and kiss the king."

"I can't, Sam. He's even uglier and smellier than you."

"You have to, Alice. Be brave. If you don't, we all die."

So Alice moved to f2 and the Caïssan king fell to the ground. Without their king the rest of the Caïssan army was powerless. Sam and Alice had worked together to defeat the alien invasion.

Sam and Alice had worked together
to defeat the alien invasion.

"I guess that makes me the smartest kid on the planet,"
said Sam.

"And I must be the bravest kid on the planet," said Alice.

*   *   *   *   *